The
SENSIBLE COOK

Arent Oostwaard and His Wife, Catharine Keizerswaard, Jan
Steen. Baker Oostwaard of Leiden proudly shows us his products:
pretzels, a *duivekater* (leaning against the wall), bread, and rolls.
Courtesy Rijksmuseum-Stichting, Amsterdam.

THE

SENSIBLE COOK

Dutch Foodways in the Old and the New World

Translated and Edited by
PETER G. ROSE

Foreword by
CHARLES T. GEHRING

SYRACUSE UNIVERSITY PRESS

First Edition 1989
99 98 97 96 95 94 93 92 91 90 89   6 5 4 3 2 1

This book is published with the assistance of a grant from the John Ben Snow Foundation.

The paper used in this publication meets the minimum requirements of American National Standard for Information Sciences — Performance of Paper for Printed Library Materials, ANSI Z39.48-1984. ∞™

Library of Congress Cataloging-in-Publication Data

Verstandige kok. English.
  The sensible cook: Dutch foodways in the Old and the New World/
translated and edited by Peter G. Rose; foreword by Charles T.
Gehring. — 1st ed.
    p. cm.
  Translation of: De verstandige kok.
  Bibliography: p.
  Includes index.
  ISBN 0-8156-0241-3 (alk. paper)
  1. Cookery, Dutch. 2. Dutch Americans — Social life and customs.
I. Rose, Peter G. II. Title.
TX723.5.N4V4713   1989   89-33457
641.59492 — dc20   CIP

MANUFACTURED IN THE UNITED STATES OF AMERICA

To
My Mother — *for the past*
Don — *for the present*
Peter Pamela — *for the future*

Born in Utrecht and educated in the Netherlands and Switzerland, PETER G. ROSE came to her special interest in Dutch cooking after moving to this country in 1964. A food teacher, historian, lecturer, and author, she contributes a syndicated column on food and cooking for the New York-based Gannett newspapers. Her research for this book on Dutch foodways took her back to her homeland as well as to numerous sites of Dutch influence in America.

CHARLES T. GEHRING, Director of the New Netherland project at the New York State Library, is translator and editor of many volumes pertaining to the Dutch in early America.

Contents

Illustrations

Foreword

I N 1609 the Dutch East India Company's ship *De Halve Maen* spent several weeks investigating the extent of the Hudson River. Although this waterway proved not to be the fabled northern passage to the Orient, Henry Hudson's explorations established the Dutch claim to a vast area between New England and Virginia. Within this colony, named New Netherland, a Dutch presence developed that was to obstruct English hegemony in North America for most of the seventeenth century.

New Netherland struggled for survival during its first three decades of existence. The Treaty of Westminster in 1654 resolved the first Anglo-Dutch war. For a decade the colony was able to attract colonists and company support as never before. As prelude to the second Anglo-Dutch war, Charles II of England decided to assert his country's desire for supremacy along the coast of North America by seizing New Netherland. Nine years later, during the third Anglo-Dutch war, the Dutch returned the favor by seizing New York and the rest of the territory that had comprised the Dutch colony. After fourteen months the region was returned to England as a result of the Second Treaty of Westminster, which ended the war in 1674.

During the tenure of New Netherland, Dutch roots were sunk deeply into the soil of the New World. This non-English presence between New England and the Chesapeake region continued to be felt both linguistically and culturally for many generations, giving the middle colonies of New York, New Jersey, Pennsylvania, and Delaware individual characteristics different from their neighbors.

Nevertheless, New Netherland has for years been neglected by historians and is said to be the best kept secret in American colonial history. Comprehensive histories of the American colonies, as well as those exclusively about New York, have devoted little space to New Netherland, and a popular history of America fails to mention it altogether.[1] This colony of the Dutch West India Company has attracted little attention in part because of the inaccessibility of primary source materials and because of the popular perception that New England should serve as the paradigm for European colonization of North America — a peculiar perception when one considers that this vast area had been home to over 10,000 persons who established a distinctive culture under the auspices of New Netherland.

Such neglect would be understandable if New Netherland were a mere historical aberration in the seventeenth century — if it had passed on leaving no historical footprints. However, this is not the case. Just as it is possible that a footprint can escape detection because it is so large, indeed, it can be argued that the impact of New Netherland on the development of America was so broad that the provenance is no longer immediately evident. In fact, this idea is nothing new. A writer in the nineteenth century speculated that if it were possible to be transported back to the seventeenth century, an American would be more at home in the world of New Amsterdam than that of Boston.[2] These influences from the past will be drawn into sharper focus when we understand the true extent of the Dutch colony of New Netherland at all levels.

When studies of the colony define the parameters of political, economic, social, and religious influences, we will be able to see how deeply they have embedded themselves into those characteristics we consider American. At present we are viewing the shape of the colony as if we were looking at a tapestry from the reverse side. We see a vague outline of form accompanied by numerous loose ends of thread, with the total concept obscured. However, the tapestry cannot be turned over at once. Slowly, as research proceeds, the work manifests itself a little at a time. The present work is an important and necessary contribution toward revealing the whole history of New Netherland, without which we cannot hope to understand what has been lying before us for so long.

Although a massive amount of source materials has survived concerning the history of New Netherland, there is little to tell us about the daily life of its inhabitants. We know that they committed all the vices still practiced today because of the court records; we know of political

---

[1]Alistair Cooke, *America* (New York: Knopf, 1973), 88.

[2]Mrs. Schuyler Van Rensselaer, *History of the City of New York in the Seventeenth Century,* vol. 1 (New York: Macmillan, 1909), 484.

machinations both internal and external because of the correspondence; we know of legal dispositions because of the notarial records. But most of what we have known about the domestic life of New Netherlanders has been gleaned from these official administrative records. Peter Rose's work changes all of that. For the first time we are presented with a primary source that offers us a detailed glimpse of domestic life. *The Sensible Cook* takes us into the kitchen where the most important dimension of daily life was focused: the preparation of food and eating.

Readers of *The Sensible Cook* are thus given both a historical and a gastronomical treat. The introduction provides new insights into the state of the art of seventeenth-century food preparation, and the recipes will provide pleasure for years to come. Although we can hope to gain only an approximation of the seventeenth-century inhabitants' outlook on life, sense of humor, and subtlety of attitude, with *The Sensible Cook* for a guide, we can at least re-create and consume what they ate and, in the process, gain entry into a daily activity that dominated their domestic life.

CHARLES T. GEHRING, Director
New Netherland Project
New York State Library
Albany, New York

Preface

As a MODERN-DAY DUTCH IMMIGRANT, I have been curious about the place of my fellow countrymen in America's past ever since I set foot here more than twenty years ago. As a cook and food writer, my main interest naturally focused on Dutch foodways and their vestiges in the American kitchen.

For years I have collected tidbits of information on the subject, but it was not until I read an article by Joop Witteveen on the history of Dutch cookbooks that the pieces seemed to fall into place.[1] In that article Witteveen discussed *De Verstandige Kock (The Sensible Cook)* and called it "really the only Dutch cookbook of the entire seventeenth century."

As part of my research I had been aware of *The Sensible Cook;* in fact, I possessed two different partial reprints. I had not seen the relevance of the book to Dutch food in the New World, however, until I read further in the text of the article and discovered a missing link. *The Sensible Cook* is only a small part of a much larger volume collectively called *Het Vermakelijck Landtleven (The Pleasurable Country Life)*.

I recognized that name immediately as one of the titles in the library at Historic Hudson Valley (formerly Sleepy Hollow Restorations) in Tarrytown, New York, where I have done a substantial portion of my research on Dutch-American foods.

The translation that follows presents the 189 recipes contained in *The Sensible Cook* and its appendixes, "The Dutch Butchering Time" and "The Sensible Confectioner," all of which are from the 1683 edition of *The Pleasurable Country Life,* held in the library of Historic

[1]J. Witteveen, "Van Trinolet tot Ragout," *Nederlands Tijdschrift voor Dietisten* 36 (1981):170–75.

Hudson Valley. The book belonged to the Van Cortlandt family.

Oloff van Cortlandt came from the Netherlands to New Netherland in 1639. He and his descendants acquired vast holdings and were among the most influential families in New York State. Grandson Pierre van Cortlandt was the first lieutenant governor of the state and also the first in the family to take up permanent residence in the Van Cortlandt Manor in Croton on Hudson, New York. In the manor house he entertained well-known figures like Lafayette, Franklin, and Rochambeau. The Van Cortlandt family lived in the house until the 1940s. After some quick ownership changes, the house was subsequently purchased in the 1950s by John D. Rockefeller, Jr., who restored it and gave it to Sleepy Hollow Restorations. The brown leatherbound copy of *The Pleasurable Country Life* was given to the organization by descendants of the Van Cortlandt family as part of a parcel of books which included several handwritten cookbooks that will be discussed in the Introduction. Unfortunately, nothing further is known of its provenance.

In order to stay as close to the original text as possible in the translation, I have sometimes had to sacrifice the flow of language but have retained, I believe, the caring warmth and especially the humor of the original. I felt it was important to reproduce the original as faithfully as possible, because I believe this book will have a mixed audience: scholars of the period, culinary historians, Dutch descendants looking further into their roots, and readers interested in cooking of any kind. When necessary I added words in brackets to clarify the meaning of the text.

One of the hardest decisions in translating this work was how to treat the unfamiliar use of slashes, as seen in the following extract from "The Sensible Confectioner":

> Boil or cook them in clear water/but not too soft or too well done/ take them from the water and let them drain/pour over it sifted finely pounded sugar until they are covered; let them stand a day/ pour off the Syrup/when it becomes thin/cook it again until [it is a] thick Syrup/then pour over the Pears again/do this as many times until the Syrup stays thick/leave them in there/they are good.

To avoid ambiguity, the slashes have been removed and, where appropriate, have been replaced with other punctuation.

In determining how to treat the author's seemingly erratic use of capitalization, I have followed the original text. At first it seemed that words were capitalized for emphasis or because they were nouns, but closer examination of the text revealed that only main ingredients were so treated. This treatment reveals something about the character of the author and his or her work. And although *The Sensible Cook* does not observe precise agreement of the pronouns, I have corrected the text only when necessary for clarity.

When appropriate, Dutch words; obscure terms and ingredients, with notes on their seventeenth-century use by P. Nijland; and weights and measures are defined in the Glossary. A further explanation of concepts and background information are given in the notes.

In the selection of illustrations, my aim was to illuminate and explain the text, but it was not possible to find paintings to illustrate all the specific items. To aid the reader in recognizing and visualizing the pastries, sweets, and baked goods, I created my own composite photo (see illustration 22).

I can now look at seventeenth-century Dutch paintings, such as the ones used in this book, only as documents of foodways. While others may enjoy the superb lighting, the composition, and other proofs of artistry, I am enthralled with the variety of vegetables, the cooking pot, or the trammel that might appear in the painting.

An economically and culturally rich republic was the cradle of *The Sensible Cook*, which represents a body of knowledge from the Dutch Golden Age. This cookbook gives us a better understanding of that period in the Netherlands, as well as new insight into the daily life of their colony in the New World.

Acknowledgments

A GRANT from the Lucius N. Littauer Foundation to translate *De Verstandige Kock* enabled me to give the work my complete concentration. I thank the Foundation for the great honor and for its faith in me. The Golden Tulip Barbizon Hotel in New York City sponsored my research trip to the Netherlands. It has been a pleasure to work with general manager Frits Bernards and his able kitchen staff on several projects that involved historically appropriate foods.

My most sincere thanks to Dr. Charles T. Gehring, Director of the New Netherland Project, for all his help and encouragement, as well as for writing the Foreword to this book.

Throughout the project my mentor and sustaining friend has been Dutch-born Dr. Elisabeth Paling Funk, a Washington Irving scholar. Together we proofread and refined the translation. She called it a *vriendendienst* (a kindness among friends); it is a kindness not likely to be forgotten. I am deeply indebted to culinary historian Karen Hess for her thoughtful comments. She allowed me to use her years of experience to benefit this book.

Everyone on the staff of Historic Hudson Valley has been extremely helpful. I would particularly like to thank the Curator and Director of Collections Joseph T. Butler and Librarian Diane J. Mansfield for the extensive use of materials.

In the Netherlands I also received welcome assistance. I would like to thank my beloved cousin E. J. von Schmidt-auf Altenstadt-Philips for her warm hospitality; Joop Witteveen for his information and advice about the history of *De Verstandige Kock;* Professor Johanna Maria van Winter of the University of Utrecht, who has shown a continued interest over the years in the subject of New Netherland foodways; and Dr. Sam Segal, who helped me immeasurably with the choice of illustrations. In addition, I sincerely thank Hilde Sels and her husband, Jozef Schildermans, in Belgium for their hospitality and advice.

I express my appreciation to all those others who helped and encouraged me: Elizabeth S. Armstrong, Daniel Berman, Elizabeth Berman, Mary A. Brown, Andrea Candee, Jacques Collen, Johannes van Dam, Christine Danowski, Dr. Charles Danowski, Cara De Silva, Meryle Evans, Liesbeth Fontijn, Howard L. Funk, A. M. van Hoorn-Jansen, Nancy Harmon Jenkins, Ruth Piwonka, Phyllis T. Riffel, Alice Ross, Consul of Economic Affairs Jan Gijs Schouten, South Salem Library, Len Tantillo, A. H. K. van Vloten, J. van Vloten-Bakker, Nancy H. Waters, Craig Williams, Nahum Waxman, Henk Zantkuyl, Dr. Nancy Zeller, and to Dr. Hans Falk in memoriam. He was an inspiration to all who knew him. A special thanks goes to all those granting permission to use the illustrations contained in this book.

The constant help, encouragement, and reassurance from my husband, Donald E. Rose, made it all possible. In our wonderful daughter, Peter Pamela, I see the continuity that is the underlying theme of this book.

The
SENSIBLE COOK

INTRODUCTION

1. *The Twelfth-night Feast,* Jan Steen. A night of merriment for everyone. A capon with a sauce and waffles are some of the foods served at this festive occasion. Note the large batter pot by the hearth. The young boy has found the bean in his bread and has been crowned king for the night. The fiddler plays, and the night's jester entertains. Carolers carrying a large star have come to the door to sing special Twelfth-night songs and will get their share of the food. The children play a traditional game of jumping over three candles. Courtesy Museum of Fine Arts, Boston. 1951 Purchase Fund.

Introduction

*T*he *Pleasurable Country Life*, of which *The Sensible Cook* forms a part, contains a wealth of information on gardening, orchards, bee-keeping, herbs, distilling, medicines, and food preservation. It seems highly probable that if Dutch settlers of the last quarter of the seventeenth century brought over any books, *The Pleasurable Country Life* was among them. It is even more likely that copies of the book were ordered from the Netherlands, as we know the settlers and their descendants were wont to do well into the eighteenth century. At the present time there are many copies in libraries all across America.

The Pleasurable Country Life consists of three main sections. In the third section we find the cookbook *The Sensible Cook* and its appendixes. Because cookbooks mostly codify already existing recipes, the knowledge gained from that book helps us understand the well-established seventeenth-century Dutch foodways in the Netherlands. It also helps us create a framework that we can fill with information about New Netherland — from a variety of sources and archeological evidence — to give us a clearer picture of a portion of America's past.

Een Notabel Boecxke van Cokerije . . . , by Thomas vander Noot, published in Brussels about 1510, is the first cookbook printed in Dutch. Together with some ten other books and manuscripts printed in the southern Netherlands, it precedes *The Sensible Cook*. Within the current boundaries of the Netherlands, however, only a few cookbooks were printed before *The Sensible Cook*, of which a work by Carolus Battus, published in 1589, entitled *Eenen Seer Schonen/ende Excellenten Coc-boeck . . .* , is really its only actual forerunner. In fact some of Battus's recipes are copied in *The Sensible Cook*, as is not uncommon in historical cookbooks.

The Sensible Cook itself has a long publishing history. It was first published in 1667, as part of a book on gardening by Pieter van Aengelen and published by Marcus Doornick. The same publisher combined it the following year, 1668, with a new gardening book written by Jan van der Groen, who was no less than the gardener to the Prince of Orange, and with a book on medicines by the medical doctor and botanist P. Nijland of Amsterdam. The collective manuscript was entitled *Het Vermakelijck Landtleven (The Pleasurable Country Life)*, which consisted of three main parts:

"The Dutch Gardener," by Jan van der Groen, starts with pictures of the beautiful gardens of royal houses in Rijswijk, Honsholredijk, Ten Bosch, and elsewhere. It continues with descriptions of trees and flowers and discusses the design of gardens and flower beds. The section ends with two hundred layouts of intricate beds, as well as arbors and sundials.

"The Sensible Gardener," by P. Nijland, gives a calendar of the cultivation of fruit trees, vegetables, and herbs and indicates how they can be used for food or medicine.

"The Medicine Shop or the Experienced Housekeeper," by P. Nijland, discusses the preparation of medicines for humans as well as animals. This third part also encompasses "The Diligent Beekeeper" and "The Sensible Cook," to which are added "The Dutch Butchering Time" and "The Sensible Confectioner," all written by an anonymous author. Some have assumed that it was the same P. Nijland, a physician, who wrote these sections. However, I agree with those who hold that a medical doctor who had written other works certainly would have insisted on having his name on the title page, especially in view of the book's popularity. It was not at all uncommon at that time for physicians to write such books.

In the form described above, more than ten editions appeared between 1668 and 1711. A 1671 edition, printed in Antwerp, contained a separate chapter on mushrooms. These were the first mushroom recipes in the Netherlands. They were written by Frans Sterbeeck, an expert in the field who later became the first author to write a scientific work on the subject. That edition also contains a helpful addition in which some of the book's North Netherlandish terms are translated for the South Netherlandish region. *The Sensible Cook* was reprinted separately in 1742 in Middelburg, Zeeland, and once more in 1802 in Amsterdam.

2. *Feeding of the Orphans,* Jan Victors. A porridge is served with rye bread and beer to drink. Note the communal dishes. In the background someone is reading from the Bible during the meal. Just as for the colleges, the meals for orphanages were carefully prescribed by their boards of directors. Courtesy Amsterdams Historisch Museum, Amsterdam.

To find out about seventeenth-century Dutch foodways we turn to Lambertus Burema. In his definitive study on the Dutch diet from the Middle Ages until the twentieth century, he cites a 1631 plan of a week's menus with seasonal variations. These menus were served to students attending the College of Theology in Leiden, and he considers them typical of the daily fare of the masses in the Netherlands at that time. Although we need to take regional differences into account, the menus give us an insight into the type of meals eaten by the less affluent.

The students ate well: on Sunday afternoon they would be given wheat bread soup, salted meat, and mutton *hutspot* (a one-pot meal) with lemons.[1] During the week such dishes as white bread soup with milk or mutton broth, salted meat, ground beef with currants, and cabbage made hearty meals. For variety the week's menu also included another kind of *hutspot,* this one with mutton and carrots or prunes, dried peas with butter or vinegar, and fresh sea or river fish. In the winter the bill of fare might feature codfish, beans, and peas, with a third course of butter, bread, and cumin cheese.[2]

Burema also cites an equally specific document of 1634, in which the mayors and city council of the city of Groningen outline the menu for a student dormitory. Meal after meal is clearly prescribed: each table for eight was to receive two pounds of stewed meat and three pounds of fried meat, which had to be good veal, beef, or mutton, according to the time of the year. Rye bread and cheese were always on the table, and pancakes as well as barley porridge were common dishes.[3]

The common meal pattern was comprised of breakfast, midday, afternoon, and evening meals. Breakfast consisted mainly of bread with butter or cheese. Beer was the usual drink not only for breakfast but also for the other meals. On the farms buttermilk was a favorite drink as well. Tea and coffee did not become popular until the end of the century. The midday meal was the main meal and seems to be the one for which the menus mentioned above were given. It generally consisted of no more than two or three dishes. The first one was often a *hutspot* of meat and vegetables; the second dish might be fish of one sort or another, or a meat stewed with prunes and currants; the third dish might be fruit, as well as cooked vegetables and *koeken* or *pasteyen* or both. On the farm this midday meal often consisted simply of a porridge, bread, and meat. A few hours after the midday meal, between two and three o'clock, some bread with butter or cheese was eaten. Just before going to bed, the evening meal was served. Again, it could consist of bread with butter or cheese, but leftovers from midday might also be served, or a porridge made from wheat flour and sweet milk might be offered.[4]

Bread was the mainstay of the diet in the Netherlands until the lat-

[1] Because of Holland's access to trade routes, the college kitchen had products available from warmer climates, such as lemons.

[2] Lambertus Burema, *De Voeding in Nederland van de Middeleeuwen tot de Twintigste Eeuw,* 114.

[3] Ibid.

[4] Ibid., 107.

ter part of the eighteenth century, when the potato started to take its place. The poor people ate rye bread; the more affluent ate bread made from wheat. As the recipes in *The Sensible Cook* show, bread was also used as an ingredient in many dishes. In addition, flour was the main component of the pancakes, waffles, wafers, *olie-koecken*, and various porridges of which the Dutch are fond. If the bread dough was prepared at home, then the bread was baked in the baker's oven; but generally bread was prepared and baked by the baker. In Jan Luiken's pictorial account of one hundred tradesmen, we find a depiction of three different kinds of bakers. He shows us the bread baker;[5] the *pastey* baker,[6] who also was the town's caterer; and the sugar baker.[7] The latter is not actually a baker, but clears and further refines the sugar and "bakes" it into the characteristic cone-shaped loaves.

Grain was not grown in the northern Netherlands (the provinces of Holland, Friesland, Groningen, and Utrecht) but was imported from the Baltic. According to Jan de Vries, during the first half of the seventeenth century, Baltic grain exports averaged 68,500 *last*, 70 percent of which was carried by Dutch ships. The *last* is equivalent to 4,772.88 pounds. The Amsterdam *last*, which was divided into 25 *mud*, became the basic unit of measure of the international grain trade equalling 3,003.6 liters, or when measuring rye, 2,000 kilograms (4,400 pounds). De Vries makes the interesting point that "relieved of the need to devote resources to grain production, the Dutch could utilize them in forms of production that gave a greater return." He goes on to say, "abundant capital could be invested in land improvements and in new equipment to produce specialized crops for which an urbanizing economy provided a buoyant demand."[8] The fact that *The Sensible Cook* uses more than twenty-five different vegetables implies that some of that money was invested in horticulture.

An expansion of horticulture was only one of the many effects of not growing grain at home. The Baltic grain trade had already started in the fourteenth century, when Dutch farmers found that the soggy soil of the Northern Netherlands lent itself better to growing grass for cattle than to growing grain. They therefore began importing the staple and,

[5] Jan Luiken, *Het Menselyk Bedryf*, 1.

[6] Ibid., 44.

[7] Ibid., 45.

[8] Jan de Vries, *The Dutch Rural Economy in the Golden Age, 1500–1700*, 171.

3. *Still Life with Beer, Bread, Cheese, Onions, and Fish,* AE van Rabel. This still life shows the typical breakfast foods: bread, cheese, and beer. Courtesy Museum voor Schone Kunsten, Ghent. Copyright A. C. L. Brussel.

in their fertile meadows, raising cattle that produced milk for the butter and cheeses for which the Netherlands became famous.

Again, the common breakfast was bread and butter or cheese, as illustrated in the still life by Van Rabel (see illustration 3). Burema even quotes a satirical poem, which he feels sums up the Dutch country people of the period (my translation):

> Curds, whey, bread and cheese
> is what he eats every day
> that's why the fellow is so dumb
> he eats more than he may.[9]

9Burema, 42.

The everyday breads had many different shapes. Some were round or oblong flat loaves baked on the floor of the oven. Others had been slashed with a razor before baking to create a characteristic V-shaped top. Rusks and white rolls were favorites as well. The shapes and names for all of these differed from region to region.

For holidays and celebrations, special breads would be baked, as for instance the *duivekater,* a diamond-shaped bread, baked from early December through the New Year. The *duivekater* appears in different forms, again according to region. In addition to the diamond—a shape apparently typical for the town of Broek-in-Waterland (see illustration 12), it is found in the shape of a shinbone (see frontispiece); and like the pretzels and sole-bread described below, it was purported to be used as a pre-Christian offering. We are fortunate that before most of the old bread forms and customs had disappeared they were recorded by J. H. Nannings.[10] His is still the main work on the subject of the meaning of bread and baked goods in Dutch folklore. He proved over and over again how bread shapes held an important place in the imagination of the people and were often an expression of their beliefs and customs.

Breads and baked goods were (and a few still are) the physical manifestations of religious and other holidays. When the molded spiced *koek* named *speculaas* appears in the baker's shop, the Dutch know the Saint Nicholas celebration is near. Three-Kings-Bread prepared for the celebration of Twelfth Night (Epiphany), contains a bean. The person who gets the piece with the bean in it is king for the night (see illustration 1).

As shown above, the breads were not only symbols of holidays but often represented a deeper meaning or took the place of earlier offerings. An excellent example of this is the pretzel. There are several explanations for the pretzel shape. In one, it was first introduced by a baker who had earned the wrath of the king by producing bitter-tasting bread and could only regain his freedom if he baked a "see-through bread." The smart baker was undaunted and created the pretzel (originally only a ring shape). In another account the word is explained through a faulty etymological interpretation of the word *jul,* which is given the meaning of wheel. According to this interpretation, the pretzel was seen as a wheel of the sun-king's wagon. The baked good was Christianized early on by having the bakers add a cross. Because of that cross, the pretzel is

[10]In *Brood- en Gebakvormen en hunne Betekenis in de Folklore.*

mentioned in manuscripts of cloister menus as early as the fifth century.

Nannings is convinced, however, that the pretzel is an offering in bread form that takes the place of the customary armring given to the dead. (In German the word *Bretzel* [pretzel] also means bracelet or armring.) There are many other examples of breads that replaced previous offerings, such as braided breads that took the place of the early offerings of hair braids at the time of the funeral, while those braids had taken the place of even earlier offerings of the widow herself. Sole-bread is another example of a bread that took the place of earlier offerings. It represents the soles of the shoes that were given to the departed to facilitate the trip to the hereafter.

Special breads were baked not only for Saint Nicholas, New Year's, Twelfth Night, Easter, and Pentecost but also for feast days like the birth of a child, weddings, and the celebration of harvest. It is clear that the Dutch who settled in the new colony of New Netherland brought with them a rich baking culture coupled to a rich folklore. We will see later on what happened to this culinary heritage.

While Burema's study tells us about the diet of the masses, *The Sensible Cook* helps us understand the foodways of the more affluent middle class households in the Netherlands. It is interesting to note that simple dishes like porridge, soup with bread, or pancakes were eaten by both classes. However, the poor people ate dried peas and beans, legumes not mentioned in the book, whereas the well-to-do could afford sugar peas (pea pods) and the other fresh vegetables mentioned in the first chapter of the book. Sugar peas are mentioned by Bonnefons.[11] In his work they are called *Pois de Hollande*, which could mean either that this kind of pea was developed in Holland or that it was at least introduced from Holland. In the households for which *The Sensible Cook* was written, servants prepared the food. Because the book addresses itself to "all Cooks, male and female," we know that both sexes worked at the hearth.

It is necessary to keep in mind that the Dutch republic was uniquely powerful and prosperous in the seventeenth century. There were many affluent households that could afford the kind of food that is discussed in *The Sensible Cook*. Compared to the neighboring countries, not only the economic status but also the republic's literacy rate was high. De Vries quotes some statistics based on signatures of brides

[11][Nicholas de Bonnefons], *Le Jardinier François*, 263–64.

4. *A Sleeping Maid and Her Mistress,* Nicholaes Maes. This painting shows us the kind of kitchenware the recipes in *The Sensible Cook* call for: a skimmer, earthenware cookpots, ladle, plates and platters, earthenware colander, and metal pots. The deep pot on the right is used to make a *hutspot*. Reproduced by courtesy of the Trustees, The National Gallery, London.

and grooms in the marriage registers of Amsterdam: In 1630, 57 percent of the grooms were literate and 32 percent of the brides; by 1660, 64 percent of the grooms and 37 percent of the brides were literate; and in 1680 figures rise to 70 percent of the grooms and 44 percent of the brides.[12] We do not know who read *The Sensible Cook*, but apparently many were able to read it. The fact that it enjoyed so many editions over such a long period of time points to its popularity.

What we can learn from this cookbook about daily life of the period can be divided into the following categories: implements employed in food preparation, available ingredients and imported goods, weights and measures, cooking methods, and typical dishes of the period. At the end of each item, I have compared it with what we know of similar practices in New Netherland in order to gain a greater understanding of daily life in the new colony as well.

With the book in hand, we can outfit a seventeenth-century kitchen for a well-to-do household. To prepare the dishes in the book, we need a stewing pan, a deep pan, a frying pan, a pancake pan, a *taert* pan, a custard pan, and earthenware pans or pots, as well as some lids for the pans. Wooden lids and also plates or platters were often used for this purpose. For roasts, we need spits with dripping pans. For the favorite wafers and soft (raised) waffles, we need an iron. A chafing dish, a *stoof*, and an earthenware pipkin or fire pot are used to cook some dishes slowly, to keep them warm, or to dry items (see illustration 4).

Knives; a cleaver; a rasp; and spoons, including a wooden and a tin spoon; a spatula; and a skimmer are implements for the preparation of the food. Though not specifically mentioned, the need for a grater and a mortar and pestle is implied. An earthenware colander, a sieve, and a drum-shaped hair sieve are mentioned for draining and straining.

Small and large bowls are necessary to hold or store foods and liquids, as are bottles and numerous pots — flat, glazed, or earthenware. The inventory includes plates, platters, cups, and glasses. These vessels are sometimes also used as a measure, for example, a cup of milk, or a half *roemer* (footed wine glass) of vinegar. Tin plates and tin bowls get separate mention in the recipes.

Miscellaneous items such as a small pin for pricking holes in walnuts to be candied and glazed tiles used for drying fruit meats must also be included; and cloth for straining or cooking, a cutting board, a

---

[12]De Vries, 116.

basin, a barrel, and a tub for pickling round out our list. In addition, although a scale is not specifically mentioned, we must assume its use because many recipes specify certain weights.

From still existing records of Frederick and Adolph Philipses' ships and New Netherland inventories, we know that the implements mentioned above were imported for the colonists. A typical ship's inventory included fire backs, fire tongues, fire shovels, mortars and pestles, various kinds of knives, frying pans, iron pots, and large quantities of earthenware. Even in the years after the English takeover, ships continued to supply all the necessities, such as wafer irons, brass mortars and pestles, bell metal pots, and earthenware.

I created my own inventory of the fruits, nuts, vegetables, salad ingredients, herbs, and flowers mentioned in *The Sensible Cook*. The list for fruits and nuts includes almonds, apples, apricots, cherries, chestnuts, currants, gooseberries, grapes, medlars, mulberries, peaches, pears, plums, quinces, strawberries, and walnuts. When I compared it to the fruits mentioned by Adriaen van der Donck in *A Description of the New Netherlands,* I found that only medlars and walnuts were missing from his list of fruits that grew both in the Netherlands and in New Netherland.[13]

I fared almost as well with my list of vegetables. According to Witteveen, what sets *The Sensible Cook* apart from a medieval cookbook is the increased use of vegetables. Sels mentions the same phenomenon in her master's thesis "De Verstandige Kok."[14] It comes as no surprise then that *The Sensible Cook* uses at least twenty-five vegetables. That number is enlarged by the use of their shoots or stems or different varieties. For example, I counted lettuce as one vegetable, whereas several different kinds of lettuces are mentioned in the recipes. My list contains artichokes, asparagus, beets, Belgian endive, Brussel sprouts, cabbage (red, white, and Savoy), carrots, cauliflower, celery, chicory or endive, cucumber, fava beans, hops, Jerusalem artichokes, lettuce, leeks, onion, parsnips, peas and sugar peas, pole or green beans, purslane, radishes, spinach, turnips, and wild chicory or dandelions. When I compared it to Van der Donck's book, the only vegetables he did not mention were cauliflower, celery, hops, purslane, and wild chicory or dandelions. In

[13]Adriaen Van der Donck, *A Description of the New Netherlands,* 67.

[14]Hilde Sels, with Jozef Schildermans, "De Verstandige Kok," *Academie voor de Streekgebonden Gastronomie,* 2:15.

addition, there was no specific mention of Belgian endive, though endive was cultivated.

I was not quite so successful with herbs and flowers. Of the thirty that are used in *The Sensible Cook*, Van der Donck mentions only half. But then he ends his description "of the Products of Kitchen Gardens" by saying that these items appeared together with "various other things on which I have bestowed no attention."[15] The herbs that appear in both books are black currant (leaves), calendula, chervil, clary, cress, fennel, laurel, parsley, rose, rosemary, sage, tarragon, and violet. Van der Donck mentions marjoram, while *The Sensible Cook* employs oregano. The two herbs are closely related.

I found only a few leftovers from medieval ways of flavoring in *The Sensible Cook*, but the use of galangal, grains of paradise, and sandalwood powder are reminders of exotic medieval methods of seasoning. Other than those, *The Sensible Cook* employs all the spices common today: cinnamon, cloves, cumin, ginger, mace, pepper, and nutmeg. It is interesting to note that the last, nutmeg, is not only used in grated form but also whole or cut into pieces.

Spices, as well as rice for recipes like the still popular rice *koekjes*, were brought in from the Spice Islands and Indonesia. Dutch seafarers and traders also brought currants, raisins, dates, lemons, bitter Seville oranges, pine nuts, Spanish capers, and wines from the Mediterranean. Sugar arrived in the Netherlands in ever increasing quantities from Brazil and the Caribbean. Simon Schama mentions that "by the 1640s there were already more than fifty sugar refineries operating in Amsterdam."[16]

We can surmise from the Philipses' ship records that like imports were brought to New Netherland. Other than the implements, we find lists of spices, raisins, and currants, but also to console some homesick Dutchman or woman there were licorice balls, a candy of which the Dutch are still fond.

There are five measures used in the recipes: the *loot*, according to Sewel's dictionary, a half ounce or about 14 grams; and the *pond*, equal to the English pound, or 454 grams. For liquid measure, the *pint* is about half a liter; and the *mengel, mengele, mengelen,* or sometimes *mingel*, is about a liter. The *mutsje* or *mutsjen* is one-and-a-half decili-

[15]Van der Donck, 67.

[16]Simon Schama, *The Embarrassment of Riches*, 165.

5. *Interior,* Willem Buytewech. Women cozily seated by the typically Dutch, jambless fireplace. One of them is frying pancakes and keeping them warm on a footwarmer. Courtesy Catalog Frederick Muller en Cie, June 1912.

ters. Information on the meaning of the different measures is scarce and inconclusive, as they seem to have varied from region to region. I confirmed the above explanations by trying them in the recipes, and they worked.

Contrary to popular belief about seventeenth-century cooking, the recipe instructions on measuring are not vague. If a *loot* is a half ounce, adding a half *loot* of cinnamon powder means a tablespoon. There are frequent instructions for a whole, half, or quarter *loot* of certain spices. This bears out Sels's belief that *The Sensible Cook* is the first Dutch cookbook to use spices with restraint so as to enhance and augment the taste of food rather than mask it.[17]

[17]Sels, 17.

The heat source for these varying modes of food preparation was the typically Dutch jambless (without sides) fireplace (see illustration 5). Though primitive on the one hand, in the sense that the heat is not as easily regulated as in a modern stove, on the other, fireplace cooking is remarkably versatile. *Hutspot,* which is cooked in a large kettle, or pancakes and waffles, which are cooked with the help of a trivet hung from the trammel (long pothook that can be adjusted up or down), are cooked directly over the fire. (There is no mention in the book of the method, but it is, of course, also possible to cook foods by burying them directly in the ashes.) Spits for roasting large pieces of meat, poultry, game, or fish, are placed in front of the fire (see illustration 13). The juices from the dripping pans are often the base for sauces, as you will see in the recipes.

Some pans have feet, others need a trivet before they can be placed over glowing coals on the hearth. Arranged that way many more dishes can cook at once than we could have bubbling away on a modern stove. Even a pot of oil for the *olie-koecken* is heated in this manner. Dishes that require heat from the top and bottom are often placed inside a larger pan (with feet or on a trivet) with a lid. The pan is placed over coals, and glowing coals are also heaped on top of the lid.

If large-quantity bread baking is done at home, it is done in a bake oven, built in a wall of the fireplace. The oven is heated only once or twice a week when the main baking is done. A brisk and lively fire is built in the oven to heat the walls completely. When the oven is thoroughly heated, the fire is removed and the oven is swept out with a wet broom. First the breads are baked; and as the oven cools down, it is used for other items. The oven is never empty until cold. To use the last bit of the heat, there is always something that can be dried (see the recipes in "The Sensible Confectioner").

Most households in the Netherlands did not have a bake oven. We know that the situation was not the same in rural New Netherland, where people did have ovens, often outside in separate small buildings to protect them from the weather. Yet in the year 1653, Beverwijck (present-day Albany) had at least six bakers, and bakers feature prominently in the ordinances and court records of other years.

A good fire is obviously the key to successful cooking. No wonder the Dutch women were so happy with the long-burning oak that they found in New Netherland, as Van der Donck describes. He tells how the new country's giant oak trees, from sixty to seventy feet high, were not only used for all sorts of farming purposes, but also made "excellent firewood, surpassing every other kind."[18] Garments made from wool and linen, which smolder rather than flare up and burn, were and are the preferred clothing for the cook who prepares food over an open fire.

An alternative to fireplace cooking was the *stoof* (foot warmer), shown in illustration 5, the pipkin with fire, or the chafing dish, as beautifully illustrated in William Kalf's *Still Life with Réchaud and Glass Decanter* (illustration 17). It aided in keeping things warm and also made it possible to stew something slowly when necessary. Another alternative to the hearth is described in *The Sensible Cook*. The brick stove in the corner of the illustration on the title page (illustration 13) is a forerunner of the iron stoves of the nineteenth century.

But what kinds of foods did patrons of this cookbook eat, and how were they prepared? The recipe section of *The Sensible Cook* begins with a "cooking register, in which most all dishes are named that one is used to preparing so that one is able to quickly think of what one wants to prepare when one is in a hurry." This sounds like the subject for an article in a contemporary magazine.

Salads, fragrant with fresh herbs and sprinkled enticingly with blue borage or orange calendula flowers would not be out of place in most modern California cookbooks. They are served with oil and vinegar or melted butter and vinegar and are eaten at the beginning of a meal. Some salads are made from fresh vegetables; for others, the vegetables are cooked, cooled, and then dressed. Asparagus is cooked briefly and eaten with melted butter and grated nutmeg, as is the twentieth-century Dutch custom. Vegetables that are served warm are eaten at the end of the meal. Notably absent are potatoes and tomatoes, but Belgian endive, sugar peas, and Jerusalem artichokes appear on the menu.

Mutton, beef, and veal are prominently featured in the *hutspot* recipes. These one-pot dishes sometimes contain just one meat and seasonings as, for instance, in "a beef *hutspot* in the Brabant manner," in which beef is slowly stewed and, when it is almost done, is seasoned with slices of ginger and crushed mace, then served with a butter sauce with chopped parsley. At other times, more than one meat or cuts of meat are cooked with a variety of vegetables. Or, at its most extravagant, the *hutspot* becomes an *olipodrigo*, and a sumptuous *olipodrigo*

[18]Van der Donck, 19.

at that, which stews to perfection thirteen different kinds of meat and finishes the dish with chestnuts, artichokes, or asparagus, as they are in season.

Game and poultry such as duck, capon, suckling pig, hare, and rabbit are served with appropriate sauces. Large fish, stuffed in some way or stuck all over with cloves, are spit roasted and finished in a stewing pot with a sauce of Rhenish wine, vinegar, cinnamon, and nutmeg. The recipe says "it is good."

Recipes for custards, creams, or fried sweets are flanked by three different kinds of pancakes. Waffles, wafers, and *olie-koecken*, one of the forerunners of the doughnut, are also part of the bill of fare. It is especially the recipes for sweets that we encounter again in the New Netherland manuscripts.

The Sensible Cook is a cookbook full of recipes that can still nourish and delight us today. What it teaches gives us a better understanding of everyday life of the period. Now armed with the knowledge from *The Sensible Cook* and the other sources mentioned above, let's look in greater detail at what happened in New Netherland.

"Dutch colonization in America was sufficiently effective that Americans today still live with details of life worked out by the seventeenth-century Dutch — cookies, Santa Claus, religious toleration, separation of church and state, caucus politics, and neighborly visits on the stoop," said Roderic H. Blackburn, former assistant director of the Albany Institute of History and Art, in a speech at the Dutch Arts and Culture in Colonial America Symposium held in Albany in August 1986. In only seven brief decades, those persistent settlers managed to entrench themselves in this country.

The early population of New Netherland was not homogeneous like the French and English colonies but consisted of people from many different countries as well as the Netherlands, an early indication of the American melting pot, as we speak of it now. A remonstrance of the West India Company, dated 1633, says that "the peopling of such wild and uncleared lands demands more inhabitants than our country can supply; not so much for want of population, with which our provinces swarm, as because all those who will labor in any way here, can easily obtain support, and therefore are disinclined to go far from home on uncertainty."[19] In addition, there was no religious persecution in the

[19]Bertus Harry Wabeke, *Dutch Emigration to North America, 1624–1860*, 14.

6. Luykas van Alen House, Kinderhook, New York. One of the sturdy Dutch houses that dot the landscape as a reminder of the New Netherland past. Courtesy Columbia County Historical Society, Kinderhook, New York. Photograph by Jake Christian.

Dutch republic and therefore no strong spiritual incentive to emigrate. It would be wrong, however, to assume that New Netherland became a dumping ground for questionable foreigners. The West India Company made sure it was served well, and undesirable individuals or those whose work was unsatisfactory were returned to the home country.

The Dutch Reformed Church in New Netherland was a unifying force in the colony. Until the establishment of the New Brunswick Seminary in 1784, its ministers were educated in the Netherlands, and they preached in Dutch. Although in later years New Netherlandish developed into a language that was quite different from what was spoken in the homeland, its use in church encouraged the congregation to retain some version of their native language and their identity.

7. Dutch Majolica Dishes, the Netherlands, ca. 1590–1650.
Dutch majolica is a tin-and-lead-glazed earthenware based on Italian designs. It predates faience, or Delft, which was inspired by Chinese porcelain. Geometric designs of various kinds were popular with potters who made Dutch majolica in the early seventeenth century. Sherds of these patterns found at New Netherland archaeological sites demonstrate that this taste carried over to Dutch New York. Courtesy Collection of the Albany Institute of History and Art.

Although at first the colony was a new-world extension of the Netherlands, it soon developed its own New Netherlandish culture. Sturdy houses, like the Luykas van Alen house (illustration 6), built by the settlers and their descendants, still dot the New York landscape. The Dutch barn is the most "European" of American barns. With its finely adzed beams, it is one of the earliest examples of barn building in the United States.

Collections in museums in New York City, along the Hudson River, and other parts of the former colony are filled with fine samples of other crafts and artistry, from beautiful portraits to painted furniture, colorful earthenware, and gleaming silver items (see illustrations

8. Standing Salt, attributed to Gaef Mendertsz, freeman 1627–
1666; City of Haarlem, the Netherlands, 1652; silver. This Netherlands standing salt was for many years in the possession of the
Hun family of Albany. It is an example of a number of Netherlands-
made pieces that have descended in New York families, some dating
as early as the seventeenth century. Silver was an important social
symbol, demonstrating not only the wealth acquired in the colony
but also close acquaintance with superior culture and the latest
fashions of the mother country. Courtesy Collection of the Albany
Institute of History and Art, gift of Mrs. John G. Hun in memory
of Dr. John Gale Hun 1964.13.

7 and 8). These items show clearly that, through imagination and hard
work, the Dutch established a good life for themselves and their descendants.

9. *Fort Orange,* L. F. Tantillo. The earliest permanent settlement of the Dutch in America. The ruins are now buried under the concrete of highway 787, Albany, New York. Courtesy L. F. Tantillo.

The excavations at the site of Fort Orange (illustration 9), the earliest permanent Dutch settlement in America, yielded fragments of Dutch majolica and other ceramics, German salt-glazed stoneware, Iberian and Italian wares, Chinese porcelain, and English earthenwares — all silent proof of the Dutch trade. Those finds can be compared to similar ones excavated at mid-seventeenth-century sites in Amsterdam. Manhattan excavations show comparable results and have aided immeasurably in our understanding and appreciation of the period.

It is not only from excavations that we can learn. Written inventories also help in the search for remnants of the Dutch past. In the inventory of the extensive possessions of Margareta van Slichtenhorst Schuyler (ca. 1630–1711), we find a brass poffer pan as well as a wafer iron. From the inventory of the belongings of Anna de Peyster (1704–74, maternal aunt of Pierre van Cortlandt, we learn that she possessed a *billabusse* pan and a waffle iron. *Billabusse, bollebuysjes, bolla-*

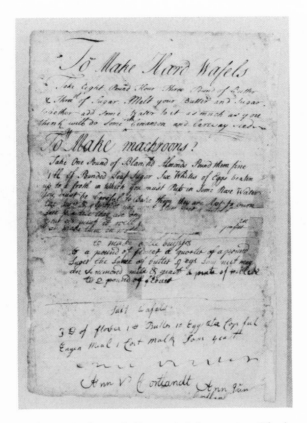

10. Typical Page in Anna de Peyster's Manuscript. The last recipe
is written in the hand of Pierre van Cortlandt. Courtesy Historic
Hudson Valley.

bouche, or *poffertjes* are different words for the same thing: tiny puffed
pancakes, made in a special pan with indentations (see illustration 23).

As an aside, for years we have been puzzled by the fact that the last
entry, a recipe for *bollabouche,* in Anna de Peyster's handwritten recipe
book is by the hand of Pierre van Cortlandt (see illustration 10). My
speculation is that Pierre inherited Aunt Anna's *billabusse* pan and obtained a recipe so that this favorite Dutch treat could be made in his
own kitchen.

Early on it was decided to outfit the colony so that it could be self-sufficient. Some members on the Board of Directors of the West India Company "had no other aim than to send their ships from here [Amsterdam] to trade in the aforesaid places [New Netherland]," but others, headed by Kiliaen van Rensselaer, persuaded them that, in addition to people to work the farms, it was necessary to supply the colony with animals, farming tools, and other implements.[20] Thus New Netherland would not only be self-sufficient but would also be able to provision the company's officials and ships engaged in the fur trade and in trade with the West Indies. Furthermore, the colony might ultimately be able to export its products to other regions, such as another new colony, Brazil.

The animals that were sent to New Netherland were well taken care of on their long trip across the ocean. Each animal had its own stall with a floor of three feet of sand and its own attendant, who received a bonus if it arrived alive.

The rapid progress of agriculture in New Netherland is shown to us in the only record of the original purchase of Manhattan. The letter written in Amsterdam, Holland, November 5, 1626, by Pieter Jansen Schagen, a deputy to the State General in the Hague, states: "High Mighty Sirs: here arrived yesterday the ship The Arms of Amsterdam which sailed from New Netherland out of the Mauritius [Hudson] River on September 23; they report that . . . they have bought the island Manhattes from the wild men for the value of sixty guilders, is 11,000 morgens in extent. They sowed all their grain in the middle of May, and harvested it the middle of August. Thereof being samples of summer grain such as wheat, rye, barley, oats, buckwheat, canary seed, small beans and flax. The cargo of the aforesaid ship is 7246 beaver skins, 178½ otter skins, 675 otter skins, [no explanation is given for the two separate entries or the half skin], 48 mink skins, 36 wild-cat skins."[21]

It will come as no surprise after reading this account that the seal for New Netherland portrays a beaver. The fur trade and economic enterprise were the motivation for life in New Netherland. Some even feel that America's commercial attitudes can be traced back to the Dutch forefathers. That New Netherland was founded specifically for the fur trade sets it apart from the other Dutch colonies of the period, which were established to produce food and related items such as pepper,

[20]Ibid., 23.

[21]John A. Kouwenhoven, *The Columbia Historical Portrait of New York*, 29.

sugar, and later on tea or coffee. Their importation had a profound and enduring impact on the diet and foodways of the Motherland.

As we also might surmise from the above account, the New Netherland colony produced its own grain. To get an idea of the importance of the different crops, we can look at the figures for the years 1642 through 1646 in Rensselaerswijck. In that period 50.8 percent of the crop was oats and 42.7 percent was wheat. However, the price ratio of wheat and oats was five to two, which makes wheat the leading cash crop. The rest of the crop was divided among barley, buckwheat, peas, and rye.[22]

It was Van der Donck who reported to the Dutch at home on how well their countrymen had succeeded in the New World. He wrote *A Description of the New Netherlands,* published in 1655, to entice his fellow countrymen to come and settle in the new colony.[23] Van der Donck, who had a doctorate in both civil and canon law from the University of Leiden, came to America in May 1641 to become *schout* (a resident officer charged with guarding the patroon's legal rights and administering justice in the colony) for Patroon Kiliaen van Rensselaer in Rensselaerswijck. He says of the new colony: "The Netherland settlers, who are lovers of fruit, on observing that the climate was suitable to the production of fruit trees, have brought over and planted various kinds of apple and pear trees, which thrive well." He proudly enumerates that peaches, plums, apricots, almonds, persimmons, cherries, figs, several sorts of currants, and gooseberries all give abundant fruit. "In short," he sums up, "every kinds of fruit which grows in the Netherlands is plenty already in the New Netherlands.[24] Garden products in the colony "are very numerous," and "the waters ... are rich with fishes."[25] He mentions that the most important fowl of the new country is the wild turkey, which is similar to the tame turkeys of the Netherlands.[26] He is

[22]Jan Folkerts, "Kiliaen Van Rensselaer and the Agricultural Productivity in His Domain: A New Look at the First Patroon and Rensselaerswijck before 1664," 10.

[23]The name of the colony was Nieu(w) Nederlan(d)t, which translates into New Netherland, singular; the translation of the title of Van der Donck's book is therefore a mistake. It was after the British took over that an "s" was added and the colony was called "New Netherlands."

[24]Van der Donck, 24.

[25]Ibid., 54.

[26]Ibid., 50

especially lyrical in his description of water fowl. In spring and fall "the waters by their movements appear to be alive with the water fowls; and the people who reside near the water are frequently disturbed in their rest at night by the noise of the water fowls; particularly by the swans, which in their season are so plenty that the bays and shores where they resort appear as if they were dressed in white drapery."[27]

To confirm the extensive use of these birds, we have the reports of the earlier mentioned excavation at the site of Fort Orange (see illustration 9). The fort was occupied continuously from 1624 until 1664; and among the items found there were many bird bones, especially from long-legged birds. Paul Huey, who was in charge of the excavation, told me that they were probably heron, among others. He also related that his findings confirmed the seventeenth-century practice of butchering by way of chopping the bones with an ax. Such a method results in large portions to be roasted, boiled, or stewed. Recipes in *The Sensible Cook* fit well into this tradition.

In the new colony, bread was not only used for the consumption of the colonists themselves but was also used for trading with the Indians. Several ordinances forbade trading baked goods with the Indians. The New Amsterdam ordinance of November 8, 1649, says in part that "through a lust and desire of great profit the Indians and barbarous natives are provided with the best in preference to the Christian Nation." The ordinance therefore forbids "selling to the Natives any fine bolled or white breads or cakes for presents."[28]

The same problems apparently occurred in Beverwijck, where on March 4, 1653, six bakers — Joannes Dijckman, Abram Staas, Rutger Jacobsz, Jan Labatie, Volkart Jansz, and Andries Herbert — petitioned the court to be allowed to sell white bread, pretzels, and cookies to the Indians; they were made to wait for a decision until members of the court returned from meeting with Stuyvesant. In an ordinance of Director and Council of New Netherland of May 30, 1653, it was demanded that Fort Orange and Beverwijck pay stricter attention to the baking ordinances, which seems to indicate that the answer was negative.[29] There is even a record of a court case in which the baker is fined

---

[27]Ibid., 53.

[28]E. B. O'Callaghan, *Laws and Ordinances of New Netherland*, 1638–1674, 112–13.

[29]Ibid., 58.

because "a certain savage" was seen coming out of his house "carrying an oblong sugar bun."[30]

Apparently, those other than professional bakers saw economic opportunity in baking for the Indians because an ordinance in Fort Orange says clearly: "And whereas it is found by experience that many, as well of this place as coming from elsewhere, in the trading season make a business to baking Koeckjens [cookies] and short weight white bread for the Indians, to the great loss of the bakers, and quit baking in the winter, the said vice-director and the honorable magistrates ordain that the bakers who quit baking after the trading season and before winter and do not accommodate the public in the winter, shall also not bake in the summer on pain of fl. 50 and the confiscation of the bread that is found."[31]

The Dutch learned how to cook some Indian dishes and fit them into their daily fare. For lovers of porridge it was not hard to get used to *sappaen,* a cornmeal mush; and the pumpkin easily fitted into a common Dutch meal as pumpkin pancakes. In his diary, Peter Kalm records eating these dishes but also tells us how the settlers and their descendants retained their typical customs and foodways. Kalm, a Swedish botanist, kept a remarkably complete diary of his travels in this country. In 1749, eighty-five years after the English took over the Dutch colony, he describes the descendants of the Dutch settlers in Albany as follows:

> Their food and its preparation is very different from that of the English. Their breakfast is tea, commonly without milk. About thirty or forty years ago, tea was unknown to them, and they breakfasted either upon bread and butter, or bread and milk. They never put sugar into the cup, but take a small bit of it into their mouths while they drink. Along with the tea they eat bread and butter, with slices of dried beef. The host himself generally says grace aloud. Coffee is not usual here. They breakfast generally about seven. Their dinner is buttermilk and bread, to which they add sugar on special occasions, when it is a delicious dish for them, or fresh milk and bread, with boiled or roasted meat. They sometimes make use of buttermilk instead of fresh milk, in which to boil a thin kind of porridge

[30]A. J. F. van Laer, *Minutes of the Court of Fort Orange and Beverwyck,* vol. 1 (Albany: Univ. of the State of New York, 1920), 242.

[31]O'Callaghan, 361.

that tastes very sour but not disagreeable in hot weather. With each dinner they have a large salad, prepared with an abundance of vinegar, and very little or no oil. They frequently drink buttermilk and eat bread and salad, one mouthful after another. Their supper consists generally of bread and butter, and milk with small pieces of bread in it. The butter is very salt. Sometimes too they have chocolate. They occasionally eat cheese at breakfast and at dinner; it is not in slices, but scraped or rasped, so as to resemble coarse flour, which they pretend [claim] adds to the good taste of cheese. They commonly drink very weak beer, or pure water."[32]

Later on in his diary he describes also how his Dutch landlady served him "an unusual salad," which "tastes better than one can imagine. . . . cabbage . . . cut in long thin strips" dressed with oil, vinegar, salt, and pepper, well mixed to evenly distribute the oil.[33]

In contrast to the frugal daily fare were veritable feasts for holidays, special occasions, or guests. Mrs. Anne Grant, of Great Britain, who lovingly and longingly recounts her youth spent with the Albany Schuyler family, describes a hospitably laden tea table:

Tea here was a perfect regale; accompanied by various sort of cakes unknown to us, cold pastry, and great quantities of sweetmeats and preserved fruits of various kinds, and plates of hickory and other nuts ready cracked. In all manner of confectionery and pastry these people excelled; and having fruit in great abundance, which costs them nothing, and getting sugar home at an easy rate, in return for their exports of the West Indies, the quantity of these articles used in families, otherwise plain and frugal, was astonishing. Tea was never unaccompanied with some of these petty articles; but for strangers a great display was made.[34]

That *The Sensible Cook* is followed by a separate section entitled "The Sensible Confectioner," with its twenty-four recipes for preserving fruits, indicates the importance of such items to the Dutch in the sev-

[32]Peter Kalm, *Travels in North America; The English Version of 1770,* 347.

[33]Ibid., 609.

[34]Anne Grant, *Memoirs of an American Lady,* 113.

enteenth century in the Netherlands. Mrs. Grant's story makes clear that Dutch descendants in New Netherland in the final decades of the eighteenth century carried on a fondness for these sweet morsels.

If that is not enough proof of the Dutch sweet tooth, listen to this lament from the seventeenth-century minister Belcampius: "Sweetness and excess is today grown so great that were they not ashamed to do so, men would found an Academy to which they would send all cooks and pasty bakers [pastry cooks] to teach them how to excel in the preparation of sauces, spices, cakes and confections, so that they should taste delicious."[35]

Washington Irving, whose *A History of New York* appeared roughly at the same time as Mrs. Grant's memoirs, treats us to an equally appetizing description of a Dutch tea table:

> The tea table was crowned with a huge earthen dish, well stored with slices of fat pork, fried brown, cut up into mouthfuls, and swimming in doup or gravy. ... Sometimes the table was graced with immense apple pies, or saucers full of preserved peaches and pears; but it was always sure to boast an enormous dish of balls of sweetened dough, fried in hog's fat, and called dough nuts, or oly koeks — a delicious kind of cake, at present, scarce known in this city, excepting in genuine dutch families; but which retains its pre-eminent station at the tea tables in Albany."[36]

It is precisely the recipes for the pastries, such as the soft or raised waffles, *olie-koecken,* and cookies acknowledged as specifically Dutch that can be traced through manuscripts. These show the continued identification with the ways of the past. The spelling for the names of these items becomes more and more anglicized as time goes on. An example is the recipe collection of the Van Rensselaers, which identifies the different recipes with the initials of the person who wrote them. We see again that the old Dutch recipes for baked goods survived. There are MVR's (Maria Sanders van Rensselaer, 1749 – 1830) recipes for tea *cookjes* and *oly cooks,* as well as her granddaughter EVR's (Elizabeth van Rensselaer, 1799 – 1835) recipes for "soft wafuls" and "pan

[35]Schama, 165.

[36]Washington Irving, *A History of New York*, 138–39.

cakes." While pancakes and waffles were part of the everyday diet, *pof-fertjes,* wafers (called *oblie* in Dutch), and *olie-koecken* were generally reserved for treats. The word *oblie* comes from the Latin *hostia oblata.* The baked good was used in churches all over Europe for the celebration of communion and later became part of secular celebrations. *Olie-bollen,* as *olie-koecken* are now called in modern Dutch, are still the traditional homemade treats on New Year's Day.

The Van Cortlandt family left several handwritten cookbooks. The oldest book belonged to Anna de Peyster. I have re-created many of her recipes in the manor kitchen. They include wafers — the Van Cortlandt kitchen has two artifact wafer irons as well as a waffle iron, *puffert* (a raised pancake), soft waffles, and *bollebuysjes.* This last recipe is that mentioned earlier, written in Pierre van Cortlandt's handwriting (see illustration 10).

A chicken recipe in the De Peyster manuscript, entitled "Butter Chicken," calls for the bird to be boiled with some mace and salt, then cut into pieces and sauteed with parsley, lemon peel, and butter. It is then gently stewed in a sauce made with some of the broth, cream and lemon juice and served garnished with lemon slices. This recipe is similar to one in *The Sensible Cook.* Her pigeons are stuffed with a farce of beef, lean bacon, "a little parcley, Swet marjoram & thime and Onion ... season(ed) with pepper and broyled on the gridiron," while basted with butter. Both are tasty dishes that we would happily eat today.

The second handwritten cookbook belonged to Anne Stevenson (1774 – 1821), wife of Pierre van Cortlandt II, and her mother Magdalena Douw (1750 – 1817). It contains two recipes for *olie-koecken,* as well as recipes for waffles, wafers, *bollabouche,* pancakes, and so forth. It also contains two different recipes for "honey cooke," another popular baked good in the Netherlands, now made only in factories. The second is a more modern version containing citron and orange peel, very much akin to a present-day Dutch version of the same *koek* (see illustration 12).

Tucked in the third cookbook with a title page marked 1865 was what seemed to be a letter because it says at the top of the page: "I feel too unwell to write, but will soon. Love to all your aff moth C. T. Beck." Among the recipes on that page is one for *puffert,* and one for *olie-cooks.* In a true adaptation to the new country's foodstuffs, the writer suggests putting "cranberries stewed very dry ... inside them."

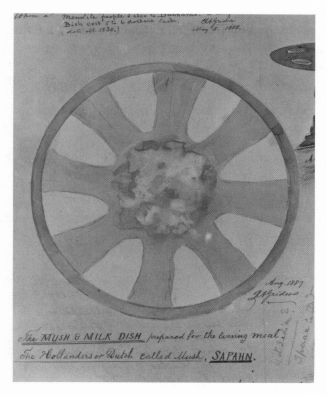

11. *Sappaen (sapahn)*, a communal dish, ready to be eaten. An illustration in Rufus A. Grider's notebook. Courtesy Rufus A. Grider Collection, vol. 8 (Schoharie Valley), p. 73 in the New York State Library, Manuscripts and Special Collections. Reproduced courtesy of the New York State Museum.

Rufus A. Grider, a teacher and artist of the Mohawk Valley, recorded his memories of Dutch life in the Schoharie Valley in 1888. In his beautifully illustrated notebooks, we find several pages with information on Dutch foodways. He relates not only that a "Mush & Milk Dish" was prepared for the evening meal, but also that "The Hollanders or Dutch called Mush Sapahn." This appears to be the same *sappaen* we discussed earlier as a dish that was learned from the Indians (see illustration 11). He then tells us how the food was served:

Until abt 1830 to 1840 the inhabitants of the rural districts of Schoharie — which were settled by the Dutch & Germans — eat their meals from a large PEWTER DISH placed by the housewife in the center of a Round top TABLE. . . . I lately measured one [a table], of 20½ in. in diameter, or 2 in larger than the head of a large barrel head. MUSH was prepared in the fall & winter of the year. — it was boiled in the afternoon & about one hour before meal time poured from the Iron Pot into the Pewter Dish & set in a cold place, cooling stiffens it. Near meal time the House Wife made as many excavations as there were guests — piling or heaping up the Centre, & filling the hollows with COLD milk . . . — as many PEWTER Table Spoons as milk Ponds were supplied. After Grace was said by the head of the family — Every one began to diminish the bank & increase the size of his White Lake by feeding on its banks and Centre — but there were limits beyond those no one could go — if for instance any one tapped his neighbors MILK POND it was ill manners — if children did so — the penalty was FINGER CLIPS.

Persons at this time do not know why such a method was practiced?

We ANSWER. Because China was scarce & high in price, & the people were poor in money — altho many had much land but little Cash. Pewter Plates cost from 50 to 75 cts each, by making such ingenious arrangements answered every purpose to save much dishwashing & labor.

facts from Mrs. Maria Sawyer   RA Grider[37]
& others.

The practice of eating from a communal dish had disappeared in most other areas in this country long before that time.[38]

He talks about other "spoon foods," such as soups, which were served frequently, he says, but also "sweet milk pap," which by now was thickened with flour rather than in the old way with stale bread. Yet "scalded milk with bits of bread" was still eaten as well, as was "Buttermilk and bread," just as related by Peter Kalm 130 years before.[39]

Sappaen apparently became such an integral part of the Dutch/American diet that it was always part of Dutch celebrations, says Mrs.

[37]Rufus A. Grider, Notebook 1888, vol. 8, 73.

[38]James Deetz, *In Small Things Forgotten*, 60.

[39]Grider, 75.

12. *The St. Nicholas Celebration*, Jan Steen. In the seventeenth century the feast of St. Nicholas was celebrated for the children only. If they had been good they received presents in their shoe, set by the chimney the night before; if they had been bad they received switches, like the boy on the left. Part of the festivities are the many special baked goods. In the basket on the left are wafers, raisin rolls, honey *koek, Deventer koek,* and *speculaas.* A *duivekater* leans against a table strewn with marzipan, candies, and *comfits.* The little girl by the chimney clutches a kind of *koek* called *taai-taai.* Courtesy Rijksmuseum-Stichting, Amsterdam.

Charles H. Hamlin in her memoirs. The former Huybertje Lansing Pruyn discusses in these reminiscences of the old Albany of her youth the celebrations of the Saint Nicholas Society, an organization "founded with the object not only of keeping the feast of St. Nicholas but also of affording relief to those of Dutch descent who were poor and in need of help.[40]

The Saint Nicholas celebration on the eve of the Saint's feast day, December 6, is so much a part of Dutch life that even during the reformation the custom could not be outlawed. The Saint had become a folk hero rather than a religious figure, and the event is a happy occasion for Protestant and Catholic alike. As shown in Jan Steen's painting *The St. Nicholas Celebration* (illustration 12), in the Netherlands the day was — and still is — highlighted by special baked goods like the *speculaas* (spiced *koek*), the Deventer *koek*, and other items, such as the festive bread symbolizing the end of the year, the *duivekater.* By the beginning of the nineteenth century, these culinary customs had changed in America, and the foods for the celebration were apparently those that had remained from the colonial past, as seen in the menu that follows.

The menu for the "supper for December 6th, 1830, at the American Hotel in Albany"[41] contained the following "National Dishes":

Suppaen en Melk	Cornmeal mush and milk
Hoofdkaas	Head Cheese
Zult	Pickled meat
Hokjes en Pootjes	Calves foot jelly
Kool Slaa Heet en Koud	Cabbage Salad, hot and cold
Rolletjes	Tripe in rolls
Worst	Sausage
Gefruyt Pens	Tripe rolled up with beef, fried
Oeli-Koeken	*Olie-koecken* or deep-fried fritters with a filling of raisins, etc.
Krulljes	Crullers

Sappaen, olie-koecken, and *krulljes* (another deep-fried baked good), as well as *Kool Slaa* (cabbage salad, our present-day coleslaw) are the

[40]Mrs. Charles S. Hamlin, "Some Remembrances," 2.

[41]Ibid., no page number.

easily recognizable remnants from the foodways of the early settlers. Because Saint Nicholas Eve is celebrated right after the autumn butchering, it apparently had become the custom in the ensuing years also to include the type of dishes associated with butchering time. We can find recipes for most of those mentioned in "The Dutch Butchering Time."

Mrs. Hamlin ends her story about the event by telling us how wines and Holland gin were also part of the celebration. Those who could not attend would send their regrets with the request that a toast be given for them. An eloquent example of such a toast was offered by Patroon Stephen van Rensselaer in 1835. The glasses were lifted to salute "Holland rescued from the sea by Dutch industry and perseverance, from Foreign usurpation by Dutch patriotism and unanimity. We honour the Brethren of that Land which they may emphatically call their own." The following year another member, one of our nation's presidents of Dutch descent, Martin van Buren, simply wished "Ever increasing prosperity to the good City of Albany and health and happiness to its inhabitants."[42]

It seems clear from the foregoing that although many descendants might have forgotten the native tongue, they had not forgotten the taste of the foods of their forefathers and continued to enjoy the pastries and other items connected with feasts and holidays not only well into the nineteenth century but to the present day. Pancakes, waffles, *oliekoecken*, pretzels, and coleslaw are some of the items that were brought to America by the Dutch colonists. Remnants from those original foodways can be found in the American kitchen today.

The next time you have a doughnut for breakfast, enjoy the crunchy coleslaw that accompanies your sandwich at lunch, or eat a cookie with your afternoon tea, you, too, will be perpetuating foodways brought here by Dutch settlers more than three hundred years ago.

[42]Ibid., 4.

THE SENSIBLE COOK,
or Careful Housekeeper

D E

VERSTANDIGE KOCK,

Of Sorghvuldige Huyshoudster:

BESCHRYVENDE

Hoe men op de beste en bequaemste manier alderhande Spysen
sal koocken/ stoven/ braden/ backen/ en bereyden; met de Saussen daer toe
dienende: Seer dienstigh/ en profytelyck in alle Hupshoudingen.
Oock om veelderley slagh van TAERTEN en PASTEYEN toe te stellen

Vermeerdert, met de

HOLLANDTSE SLACHT-TYDT.

Hier is noch achter opgevoeght/ de

VERSTANDIGE CONFITUURMAKER,

Onderwysende/ hoe men van veelderhande Vruchten/ Wortelen/ Bloemen en Bla-
den/ etc. goede/ en nutte Confituren sal konnen toemaken/ en bewaren.

t'Amsterdam, By GYSBERT de GROOT, Boeckverkooper tusschen de
twee Haerlemmer-sluysen in de groote Bybel. Met Privilegie.

13. Title Page of *De Verstandige Kock*, 1683 edition. A view of a
busy seventeenth-century kitchen. In the left corner is the stove, for
which building instructions are given in the book. The spits by the
fire have dripping pans, from which the liquid is used later for
sauces. In the other corner a brick bake oven is being heated for
baking. The two cooks are hard at work. One is filling yet another
spit, while the other is preparing pastry shells. Note the peacock
pastry shell in the foreground. Courtesy Historic Hudson Valley,
photo by Wally McFall.

facing page:

[1]The word *verstandig* in the Dutch title can be translated in many ways: smart, clever,
knowledgeable, wise, understanding, skillful, intelligent, even the old English word
nimble-witted, as well as sensible. After a great deal of deliberation I decided on *sensible* as the word that came the closest to the intention of the author.

[2]"In the Large Bible" means "under the sign of the Large Bible." On the market square
in Delft, there is still such a house with a large Bible sign over the front door.

THE
SENSIBLE[1] COOK,

or Careful Housekeeper

DESCRIBING,

How to cook, stew, roast, fry, bake and prepare all sorts of Dishes in
the best and most able manner; with the appropriate Sauces:
Very useful and profitable in all Households.

Also to prepare many kinds of CAKES and PASTRIES.

Enlarged, with the

DUTCH BUTCHERING TIME.

To which is added the

SENSIBLE CONFECTIONER,

Instructing how to prepare and preserve good and useful confections from
many kinds of Fruits, Roots, Flowers, and Leaves, etc.

In Amsterdam, at Gijsbert de Groot, bookseller between the
two Haarlem sluices in the Large Bible.[2] With Privilege.

Extract from the Privilege [to print and sell].

I N A GRANT dated December 10, 1661, the Gentlemen of the Provincial Council of Holland and West Frisia allow Marcus Doornick, Book seller in Amsterdam, for a period of 15 consecutive Years, to solely print and sell a Book named *The Pleasurable Country Life* consisting of three parts: first, "The Sensible Gardener"; second, "The Dutch Gardener," decorated with curious Prints; third "The Experienced House-keeper," together with "The Sensible Cook" etc., prohibiting anyone else in any other Language to Reprint or Sell whole or in part, in large or small Size, at such fines and penalties, as is included in the larger grant.

Was signed

JOHAN de WITT.

By the order of the States,

HERBERT VAN BEAUMONT.

Afore-mentioned Privilege I have assigned with all its appurtenances, to Michiel de Groot, book seller. Actum in Amsterdam June 30, 1677.

MARCUS DOORNICK

facing page:

³This register is not a table of contents but a reminder to hurried cooks, who were just as rushed three hundred years ago as they are today, and for whom thinking of what to prepare was just as difficult.

⁴Most of us tend to believe that Belgian endive is a recently developed vegetable, but the Dutch description is so clear that we must assume that Belgian endive was used in the seventeenth century.

⁵To people already used to eating such a large variety of birds, it must have been reassuring to find the abundance of birds in New Netherland.

Cooking Register[3]

In which most all Dishes are named that one is used to preparing, so that one is able to quickly think of what one wants to prepare when one is in a hurry.

About Salad.

Head lettuce	Wild chicory or
Endive	dandelions
Leaf lettuce	Beetroots
Lamb's Lettuce or	Chicory roots
Corn Salad	Red cabbage
Hops salad	White cabbage
Shoots of Endive	Onion, boiled or
roots[4]	fried

About all sorts of greens, to stew.

Spinach	Celery and
Beet, Head Lettuce	Asparagus
Endive	Pot Herbs
Sorrel, Borage	Artichokes
Bugloss, *Rumex*	
Patientia [a kind of sorrel]	

About Meat.

Beef	Sweetbreads
Veal	Feet
Mutton	Meatballs
The Heads	Hamballs
Midriffs	Spanish *hutspot*
[diaphragm]	

About Game.

Hare	Roebuck
Rabbits	Suckling pigs
Wild boar	Roe, Deer

About Poultry.[5]

Peacocks, Swans	Plover, Thrush
Heron	Quail
Bitterns	Lark
Snipes, Turkeys	Starling
Wild Geese	Finch
Geese, Pheasants	Hens, Capons
Black Grouse	Pigeons
Partridge	Ducks
Woodcock	Widgeons
Watersnipes	Pintail ducks
Lapwing [Peewit,	Teal
Green Plover]	

About salted, smoked and dried Fish.

Salmon	Herring
Haberdine	All sorts of
Haddock	Stockfish
Shad	Bloater
Mackerel	Sprat

About sea-fish.

Cod	Sole
Lean Codfish	Dab
Haddock	Plaice
Halibut	Herring
Turbot	Sardine
Whiting	Shad
Whiting	Lobster
[Molenaar: *Gadus*	Crab
merlangus]	Oysters
Weever	Mussels
Cormorant	
Ray [Koch: misprint of *Rogh*]	

About River Fish.

Sturgeon	Tench
Salmon	Roach
Pike	Flounder
Barbel	Gudgeon
Carp	Eel
Bream	Eel-pout
White Bream	Smelt
[Blay: archaic	Shrimp
spelling of *Bley*]	Lampreys
Bass, Perch	

About Baked Goods.

Olie-koecken	Omelets
Buckwheat	Pudding
Koecken	*Vlayen* [open-
Pan Cakes	faced pies, or
Waffles	custards]
Wafers	Spanish Porridge
Kucheltjes [not	Blanc Mange
located; perhaps	Raised Pan Cakes
kogeltjes: small balls or bullets]	

About *Taerten*.

Almond-*taert*	Cream-*taert*
Apple-*taert*	Quince-*taert*
Pear-*taert*	Meat-*taert*
Cherry-*taert*	Calfs-tongue-*taert*
Currant-*taert*	Marrow-*taert*
Gooseberry-*taert*	Bread-*taert*
Chervil-*taert*	

About *Pasteyen*.

Meat *pastey*	Oyster *pasteyen*
Roasted Rabbits,	Lemon *pasteyen*
Hares, Turkeys	Sweet *pasteyen*
Roasted Chickens	
Roasted Pigeons	

How to make a useful Stove.

Before the Cooking is demonstrated, it seems a good idea to the Sensible Cook to describe to the Reader the form of a useful Stove. Such a stove, on which one can cook and stew with little fire, is not only necessary but also very useful in a household, provided one has the opportunity to install one or space by the fire or in one corner or another of the hearth. The form of this stove is as follows and is shown to the reader on the title page: The bricks are laid in a square or round shape, high 3 or 4, and wide 2 feet. In the top is a round hole, wide 8 or 10, deep 6 or 8 inches, which is narrower on the bottom than on top to give more heat. On top of this an iron grate is placed to hold the fire. In order not to extinguish the fire the hole is surrounded by three iron knobs, protruding to a height of about 1 ½ inches on which the pots rest. Because the brickwork almost burns up through the great heat, some make an entire iron lining of 6 to 8 inches deep, narrower at the bottom than at the top. The grate is placed at the bottom of the lining; the iron knobs are attached at the top. Next the brickwork is finished all the way around, except on the side of the hearth where an iron door is inserted so that one is able to remove the fallen ashes. In this iron door a smaller door is constructed to regulate the air. This small door is opened when something is cooking; the fire will start to glow and gets air to burn.

Some who have large households make the shape of the stove so big that 4 or more pots or dishes can boil or stew at the same time. This stove is constructed as explained above. Each round hole has a grate underneath, but the stove only needs one door for the fallen ashes. In the ashes, one can place a loose little grate that will sink in only 3 or 4 inches, so that if one wants to heat or stew something, this can be done with little fire.

COOKBOOK.

To all cooks, male and female.

The Sensible Cook warns all cooks to know better than to add all sorts of strong and sweet French Wines to the Sauces, because Wines like *Lagonse, Hooghlantse* and *Haentjes* wines later change all their sweetness to bitterness (as soon as they are warmed over the fire) and spoil therefore the Sauces to which they are added.[6] However, for those Sauces in which one wants to use Wine one should only take Rhenish Wine; or, otherwise, if this is not available take fermenting French Wines, which means they are acidy, such as *Tossaense,* Cognac, or *Coutouwe* wine, and also Red Wine François. But the Sensible Cook rejects the use of all Wines in Sauces and says that they can be made more ingeniously, more pungent, more savory and tastier with water, Vinegar, Lemon juice and Verjuice,[7] everyone to her own demand.

---

[6]As in the first sentence of the description of the stove, *The Sensible Cook* changes suddenly from a book title to a person, and an opinionated person at that. He or she instructs us about the "useful stove" and cannot help but admonish us about the use of French wines in sauces. It is amusing to find that, in spite of this admonition, he or she frequently employs wines in the sauces. The cook also adds little editorial comments at the end of recipes and informs us that the dish "is good" or "very tasty" or, better yet, "delicious." Then again it sometimes just "tastes all right."

I offer the following possible explanations for the kinds of wines mentioned in the paragraph:

Lagonse—from the Lago Maggiore

Hooghlantse — either a German wine or from the Haagland, a wine area near Leuven in present-day Belgium

Haentjes—from the (Rhine) wine area between Karlsruhe and Worms

Tossaense—from Tuscany

Coutouwe—from Couthuin, a small village near Huy, an old wine area in present-day Belgium

[7]Verjuice is the juice of unripe grapes. It is used to accent the flavor of the other ingredients. Substitute wine vinegar; use a teaspoon at a time.

of Sorghvuldige Huyshoudſter.   63

hart gekoockt / en murruw gewreven daer onder.

Om Savoy-kool naer de Spaenſche manier te prepareren.

Neemt Savoy-kool / naerſe wel murruw is geſoden / en in kleyne ſtucrkens in de ſchotel gelept / voort warm Hamele-ſop met wat Peper op-gekoockt / daer over gegoten / als dan wel Olie van Olijven en Sout over gedaen / is ſmakelijck en goet.

Van Aſpergies.

Aſpergies worden ſlechts ghekoockt / niet al te murruw / en dan gegeten met Olie / Azijn / en Peper / of anders met geſmolten Boter en geraſpte Notemuſkaten.

Diverſe manieren om Artiſocken te ſtoven als die wel gaer geſoden zijn.

Neemt wat Azijn en ſchoon Water /

Boter en geſtooten Peper / Noten / en ee 1 weynigh geſtooten Beſchuyt en Suycker / laet dit ſoo ſamen door ſtoven.

Een ander manier.

Als de Artiſocken wel gaer geſoden zijn / neemt een platte pot / doet 'er wat Hamele-ſop in / met een ſcheutje Rhenſe Wijn / Peper / Foelie / Noten / wat ſijn geſtooten Beſchuyt / een weynigh Sout en Boter / ſet 'et te ſtoven met de Artiſocken. Ook ſtooft men die wel met krupm van een oubacken Witte-broodt in roode Wijn geweeckt / kleyn gewreven / en dan daer een weynigh Azijn in / en naer behooren Suycker / Caneel / Noten Peper en Boter. Men eet oock Artiſocken als ſy gaer geſoden zijn met een ſaus van Boter en Azijn / en Peper of Olie : en Azijn / Peper en Sout voor Salaet.

Van alderley Vleeſch.

Om Schapen-vleeſch te ſtoven.

Neemt Schapen-vleeſch in groote ſtucken gehackt / wel gekoockt en geſchupmt / doet 'er by lange ſtucken van Pingſternakelen / en voorts allerley Moes-krupdt grof gehackt / en wat Peper en Sout ; dit ſoo t' ſamen kokende en ſtovende / tot het Schape-vleeſch wel gaer is / dan met ſop en al op geſchept / in een Schotel / daer te vooren Terwen-broodt in geſneden is.

Om een Kalfs-ſchinckel met groen Kruyt te ſtoven.

Als 't vleeſch wel geſchupmt en wat Sout daer in gaer is / doet 'er dan het geſcherfde krupt op van Kervel / Biet / en wel Suring / een hant vol of twee Sirupf-krupt / en wel Boter / is goet.

Om geroockt Vleeſch met Eyeren te roeren.

Scherft het Vleeſch ſoo kleyn als ghy kunt / doet 'et in de pan met Boter / laet 'et heet werden / dan daer Eyeren by met Peper / en ſoo onder een geroert. Men doet 'er oock wel wat Comijn over.

Om een Spaenſe Huſpot te maken.

Neemt Schapen ofte Kalfs-vleeſch / laet in ſtucrkens hacken / als een lidt van een dupm / geſchupmt zijnde / laet 'et wel murruw koken / dan daer Boter en gehackte Peterceﬁe by doende / laet 'et noch eens op koken / opgeſchept zijnde / neemt men 2 of 3 doren van Eyeren / in ﬂamoen-ſap kleyn geklopt / daer dan over gedaen / is heel ſmakelijck.

Om:

14. Typical Page in *De Verstandige Kock*. Courtesy Historic Hudson Valley, photo by Wally McFall.

About Salad, Pot Herbs, Herbs for Boiling and Stewing, Fruits from Garden and Earth.

To prepare raw Salads.

ake Head Lettuce, Leaf Lettuce, Curly Lettuce, Lamb's Lettuce, also the shoots of the Dandelions or wild Chicory, also the shoots of Chicory roots, Endive, or red and white Cabbage or Cucumbers, whatever one has on hand that is best or that is in season and all well cleaned is eaten with a good Oil of Olives, Vinegar, and Salt. On some [vegetables] additional herbs are used according to everyone's desire, but the usual are Cress, Catnip, Purslane, Burnet, Rocket, Tarragon, Buttercup, one may also add the flowers of Bugloss, Borage, Rose, and Calendula. This salad is also eaten with melted Butter and Vinegar gently heated together instead of Oil and Vinegar, according to everyone's desire.

To prepare Salad from Celery.

Take Celery, clean it, and pull the tip of the knife through the heads, then place it in cold water. It will curl nicely. Eat with Oil, Pepper, and Salt. Some take Vinegar or press out a fresh Lemon over it.

To prepare a Salad of Artichokes.

Take Artichokes, clean the leaves of all impurities so that the bottom is clean, cut into pieces. It is eaten with Pepper, Salt, Sugar, Oil, and Vinegar. Radishes[8] are washed, scraped, and eaten with salt only.

To prepare all kinds of cooked Salads.

Take the hearts of Head Lettuce, cooked just a little, or Chicory roots or Beetroot or Beets or stems of Purslane or stems of Beets after they

---

[8]I do not know why the instructions for radishes immediately follow those for artichokes. Maybe they were equally common? It appears that both were eaten raw.

have been peeled properly or young Green or Pole beans[9] cooked until done or shoots of Hops, shoots of Elder, Onion, or Leeks; also red or white Cabbage cut fine and cooked a little while, everyone to his appetite and all of it well done. [These salads are] prepared with Oil of Olives, Vinegar, Salt, Pepper; for some [vegetables] one takes also Sugar or Currants according to taste.

To stew Sugar Peas.

Take Sugar Peas, string them, and place them in a flat [shallow, earthenware] pot, add a little water, shake frequently, add Butter, let it stew together. Sometimes green parsley is added, cut fine. Is very good.

To stew Summer-turnips.

Take Turnips which have been cut into strips, then place them in a flat [shallow, earthenware] pot with half a small bowl of water. Let them stew a bit with Butter and often shake them.

To stew Summer-turnips in another manner.

Take the Turnips when they are cut, boil them first with water. When they are almost done then strain them on an earthenware colander. First the Butter is melted with a little Sugar then the Turnips are added and shaken together. Is good.

[9]The original text talks of "Turkish or climbing beans," which seems to indicate green or pole beans. We might surmise this not only from the recipe, which calls for "Turkish Beans cut up," but also from a previous section in the collective work entitled *The Sensible Gardener*. In his gardening calendar, the author, P. Nijland, describes "Turkish beans" as "green beans." Van der Donck has this to say on the subject: "The Turkish beans, which our people have introduced there grow wonderfully; they fill out remarkably well and are much cultivated. Before the arrival of the Netherlanders, the Indians raised beans of various kinds and colours, but generally too coarse to be eaten green." (Van der Donck, 71.)

To stew Fava beans, Pole, or Turkish [Green] Beans.

Take Fava or Turkish [Green] Beans cut up. When they are cooked until done, then drained, take chopped Parsley with Butter and Salt, a spoonful or two of Mutton Broth, add them together in a pot so it can cook a bit, then add the Beans, shake often. Sometimes some Savory is also added, everyone to his own desire.

To cook Pot-Herbs.

Take clean Well-water, add one or two stale round White breads, depending on how much you want to cook, hang it [the pan] over the fire. In the meantime cut the Pot-Herbs: Chervil, Beet, a few blades of Mace, Borage, or Bugloss, the first tiny leaves of the black Currants and of Calendulas, also Leek and Catnip, a little Spinach, but not Sorrel that would make it too greyish [in color], when it [all] is cut up fine and the water and bread have boiled for a while until it [the bread] has dissolved. Add [the Pot-Herbs] to it and let it boil until done then Butter and Salt as you desire.

To stew all sorts of Greens.

One takes Spinach, Head-Lettuce, Endive, Beet [greens], Sorrel or Brussels Sprouts or Purslane; each cooked until well done, is stewed with Butter, Mace, Nutmeg, and Salt.

To make a Chervil soup.

Carefully pick over and cut the Chervil fine, cook it in Sweet-milk until it is done, add 2 or 3 Eggs, and a good piece of Butter, but with the Eggs and Butter it should not boil. Cut White-bread in a dish and pour it [the soup] over it.

To make Currant soup.

Take red Currants, strip them from the stems, take Rhenish wine, a little water, and a little Butter, sweeten with Sugar, then place White-bread in a dish, pour [the soup] over it so that the bread gets soggy, and then sprinkle with Sugar and Cinnamon.

To stew Cauliflower and Savoy cabbage.

One takes Cauliflower or Savoy cabbage after it has been cleaned and cooked until well done and stew it with Mutton-broth, whole Pepper, Nutmeg, Salt, without forgetting the excellent Butter of Holland. A hardboiled egg yolk which has been rubbed fine is sometimes placed underneath. [Literally in the text: "underneath," but probably over the head of cabbage, as is still done today.]

To prepare Savoy cabbage in the Spanish manner.

Take Savoy cabbage after it has been cooked until well-done and has been cut into small pieces and placed into the dish, then cook together warm Mutton broth and some Pepper, pour it [the broth] over, as well as Oil of Olives and Salt. Is tasty and good.

About Asparagus.

Asparagus are just boiled, not too well-done, and then eaten with Oil, Vinegar, and Pepper or otherwise with melted Butter and grated Nutmegs.

Different ways to stew Artichokes when they are cooked until done.

Take some Vinegar and clean Water, Butter and crushed Pepper, Nutmegs and a little crushed Rusk and Sugar. Simmer these together.

15. *The Vegetable Woman,* Joachim Wttewael. Artichokes, cabbages, carrots, onions, apples, small cucumbers, grapes, berries, cherries, and nuts fill this vegetable stall with multiseasonal abundance. You will find recipes for all of them in *The Sensible Cook.* Courtesy Centraal Museum, Utrecht.

Another way.

When the Artichokes are boiled until done, take a flat [shallow, earthenware] pot, put some Mutton-Broth in it, a dash of Rhenish Wine, Pepper, Mace, Nutmegs, some finely crushed Rusk, a little Salt and Butter, stew it together with the Artichokes. They are also stewed with crumbs from a stale White-bread which has been soaked in red Wine, finely mashed, and then a little Vinegar added and Sugar, Cinnamon, Nutmeg, Pepper, and Butter as appropriate. Artichokes are also eaten after they have been boiled until done with a sauce of Butter and Vinegar and Pepper or Oil: And Vinegar, Pepper, and Salt as a Salad.

About All Sorts of Meat.

To stew Mutton.

Take Mutton; cut into large pieces, well cooked and skimmed, add to it long pieces of Parsnips, and furthermore all sorts of greens coarsely chopped, and some Pepper and Salt; thus cooking and stewing these together until the Mutton is done. Serve with the broth in a Dish in which Wheat bread has been cut beforehand.

To stew a Knuckle of Veal with green Herbs.

When the meat is skimmed and cooked until done with some salt in it, add to it the cut greens of Chervil, Beet, and also Sorrel, a handful or two of *struyfkruyt*[10] and also Butter. Is good.

To stir smoked Meat with Eggs.[11]

Cut the Meat as small as you can, place it in the pan with Butter, heat it, then add Eggs with Pepper and stir together. Some sprinkle it with Cumin.

To make a Spanish *Hutspot.*

Take Mutton or Veal, have it cut into pieces the size of a thumb's knuckle, after it has been skimmed, let it cook until done, then add Butter and chopped Parsley. Bring it back to a boil. Once it has been dished up take 2 or 3 Egg yolks beaten in Lemon juice, pour it over the dish. Is very tasty.

[10]*Struyfkruyt* was not located. *Struyf* means the content of an egg; *kruyt* means herb. Marjoram is a favorite herb to use with eggs and also has egg-shaped leaves. I speculate therefore that marjoram is meant in this case.

[11]"To stir smoked Meat with Eggs" is another one of those timeless recipes. We can recognize it as chipped beef and only need to add the toast to get a popular modern dish.

To stew a Hen with Greens.

Take a good Hen which has been cleaned well, boil it with some pieces of Mutton and a little Salt. When it is half done add in a stewing pan some sausages or small Meatballs, also a good handful of Endive, Salad greens, Sorrel, and Celery also Asparagus. Especially do not forget the Butter.

To stew a Hen with Sorrel.

When your Hen is almost done take Sorrel which has been washed clean with some whole blades of Mace and whole Pepper then [add to these] a salted Lemon[12] cut into slices and cooked until half done [and] combined with all the above and thus let stew [all] together with Butter and Verjuice. Is very good; if you wish, add Sausages and little Meatballs. Is not bad.

To stew a Hen with Rice.

After the Hen has been cooking in the stewing pan until half done add Rice with Mace and some Pepper. When it is almost done add slices of salted Lemons and Butter.

To make a Hen with Cauliflower, or ordinary *Olipodrigo.*[13]

Take a Hen, boil it until almost done and then Cauliflower also almost done and Jerusalem Artichokes[14] also cooked, Mutton also almost

[12]Lemons were salted to preserve them. Salted lemons are still in use, for instance, in the Moroccan kitchen.

[13]A popular dish all over Europe was the Spanish *olla podrida*, or as it is called in Dutch, *olipodrigo*. We find recipes for it in English and Dutch as well as in French cookbooks (Karen Hess, *Martha Washington's Booke of Cookery*, 86 and Barbara Ketcham Wheaton, *Savoring the Past*, 33). The recipe seems to indicate that the object was to impress the diners with the abundance of its ingredients. For the Dutch it was only an extension of their more modest *hutspot*.

[14]In the original it says *artisocken onder de aert*, which translates as "artichokes under

done, Pigeons also almost done, Endive also, Sheep feet also, Celery also, but each cooked separately. Take your stewing pan and add all to it, stew it until almost done, add small Meatballs, Sausages, Mace, Nutmeg, Pepper, and also Butter. Let it stew together until it is done: while dishing it up add Verjuice, Lemon juice, or fresh Lemons. Carefully sprinkle the rim of the dish with crushed Rusk.[15]

To make a Pullet Fricassee.

Take a young Hen, some strip off the skin, wash it clean, and chop it into pieces the size of about half a finger, place it in a flat [shallow, earthenware] pot and amply cover with water, well skimmed, and then add some Salt and a little whole Pepper and thus let it boil until it is done. Drain off most of the broth, add Butter and minced Parsley and some crushed Mace or Nutmeg and let it fricassee stirring frequently. Then take Lemon juice and 4, 5, or 6 Egg yolks beaten and some of the same broth that was drained off, stir it together, pour [the mixture] in the pot with the Hen on the fire, stir steadily so that it stews together and then immediately place it from the pot in a dish and chopped Parsley sprinkled on the rim [of the dish].

To stew a Hen with Orange peels.

Take a Hen, roast it almost done, take it from the spit, take Orange peels cut into quarters, boil them in water until done, take a clean pot, Rhenish wine, add the Orange peels and Sugar to make it sweet, add the Hen, let it stew until it is enough. Dish up together and sprinkle with cinnamon powder.

the earth": Jerusalem artichokes therefore, rather than the green thistle variety. From a 1621 ode to that vegetable by the Dutch botanist Pieter Hondius, in which he gives it the same name, we know that Jerusalem artichokes were grown in the Netherlands.

[15]In this recipe as in some that follow we are told to present the food with rusk, chopped parsley, oregano, or a mixture of rusk, chopped parsley, and hardboiled egg yolk, sprinkled on the rim of the platter. Try it. It creates a nice, finished presentation. To make the garnish stick, rub the rim with butter first.

16. *Kitchen Scene,* Hendrick Sorgh. As we saw in *A Sleeping Maid and Her Mistress,* illustration 4, in this painting we also find many cookware items: large cooking pots with or without feet, pitchers, platters, and the typical lobed bowl (center in front of the tub). Note how a barrel is used as a table. Meats are hung on the domed device at the ceiling, which can be moved up or down by way of the pulley attached to the side of the hearth. Courtesy by permission of the Earl of Mount Charles, Slane Castle, Ireland; photograph Courtauld Institute of Art, London.

To prepare a Lemon-heart.[16]

Take minced Veal just like for Meatballs, add to it Nutmeg, Pepper, and Salt as well as peels of a fresh Lemon cut into small pieces, for each

[16]Presentation is also improved when meats are shaped attractively. Heart shapes were popular, as we'll learn from this recipe and others, in which well-seasoned veal is padded into the shape of a heart and fried whole.

pond of meat an Egg yolk, a crushed Rusk and mix it all together, shape it in the form of a large Meatball or in the form of a Heart, stew it with little water. When done take off the fat, add Verjuice, Butter, and peels of a salted Lemon which has been boiled in water first. Let it come to a boil together, then dish up; a sauce is poured over made from Verjuice beaten with Egg yolks.

To stew Hens and Pigeons with Bacon.

Take green excellent Lovage[17] with bacon chopped fine, Pepper, Ginger, and Clove-powder with it, place that in the Belly [of the Hen or Pigeon], lard them also with Bacon and stew them in Water and butter, add Spices, let it thus stew until it is enough. Before you dish it up add some Rhenish wine or Vinegar and bring it to a boil for a moment.

To stuff Pigeons.

Take Parsley and cut it fine and stir in an Egg and Butter, Ginger, Sugar, and Currants, place this in the Pigeon.

To nicely cook young Hens, Turkeys or Ducks.

When they are cleaned inside and washed fill them and cram them full with Parsley. Boil them then only with Salt and Water until they are done. Take an earthenware pan, pour in some Verjuice and Salt [and butter], and when the butter is melted take out the Parsley from the Hen, cut it [the parsley] small, add it to the Verjuice and Butter, stir them together well, place in a Dish and the Hen or Duck whatever it may be on it. Is absolutely delicious.

[17]Lovage is called in Dutch *vleesch-kruyt:* meat-herb. In modern usage it is also re-ferred to as "Maggi-plant" after the popular European condiment Maggi, which is added to sauces and soups whether they need it or not. The herb, which once estab-lished in the garden becomes a large plant, has a flavor somewhat stronger than celery. In our text, it is used not only with meat, but also with poultry and fish.

To prepare young live [meaning, freshly killed] pigeons
in an hour and a half.

Take Pigeons which have had their necks cut off, place them in a bucket of cold Rain water, after they have been in it for a large half hour scald the feathers with hot water. After they have been cleaned cut them in pieces and then they are boiled in a deep pan with water for an hour and a half. When the water is drained off fry them in Butter,[18] pour on a sauce [made] from Butter, cut parsley, egg yolks with Verjuice, Mace, and Nutmegs, *Probatum est.* [It has been approved.] Hens, Capons, Turkeys, Rabbits, and Pheasants as well as others that are young can be prepared in the same manner.

To stew a whole haunch of Mutton.

Take a whole haunch of Mutton which has been cooked until well-done, place it in a stewing pan, add salted Lemon (cut into slices), some Mace, Butter, Nutmeg, and grated White-bread and Egg yolks. Some also add chopped Parsley.

To prepare a pickled [salted] whole haunch of Mutton
in the English manner with a Sauce.

Take Parsley, cut it fine, add it to some Butter, let them cook for a moment and add an eighth of a *pond* of Spanish Capers and some Pepper, stir it together. It is a good sauce to dunk Meat into.

To stew a whole Sheep's-haunch, or *Hutspot* with Artichokes.

When the Meat is done, pour off a portion of the broth with the fat and add to it the stem of the Artichokes (which first have been cooked in water until well done) with a good piece of Butter and some whole Pepper and Mace and let it thus stew together.

[18]The common cooking practice was to boil the food first and then fry it; or roast it first and then finish it in the stewing pan.

To stew a whole Sheep's haunch, or *Hutspot* with Asparagus.

When the meat is done take off the fat completely, take Stewing asparagus, break off the tender parts in small pieces and washed clean add
them to the meat and thus cooked in the broth. When it is done add Butter and a few pieces of Nutmeg,[19] let it thus stew and then [it is] eaten
with spoons; some add Lemon or a handful or two of Sorrel; if one
wants to stew whole Asparagus to serve on the dish then the Asparagus
have to be boiled in water first until almost done and then added to the
meat after the fat has been skimmed from the broth.

To make a sauce for a boiled whole haunch of Mutton.

A well-cooked Sheep's Haunch. Take some Parsley cut fine, a crushed
Rusk, some Sugar and Vinegar stirred together, serve separately in a
sauceboat. Is very good and pleasant to eat with it.

To make Meatballs.

Take veal with Veal-fat chopped, add to it Mace, Nutmeg, Salt, Pepper,
knead it together, then you can make [meatballs] from it as large and as
small as you please, also all of it is fried in the pan as one large meatball;
many take a few of the outside peels thinly pared of Oranges or Lemons,
cut very fine. It gives a very good smell and flavor.

To make Meatballs without casing.

Take chopped Veal, crushed Pepper, Mace, Nutmeg, some crushed
Rusk, Eggs, but leave out half of the whites of the Eggs, knead it together
and make oblong Meatballs, roll them in the Egg white and when the
water boils add them to the pot to cook them until done, then fry them
in Butter. Are very good.

[19]Nutmeg is frequently used in the recipes. I assume that in general it is grated (see the
nutmeg grater in Willem Kalf's painting, illustration 17), unless otherwise specified as
it is in this and other recipes where we are told to use nutmeg, whole, cut in half, in a
few pieces, or, more specifically, in four or six pieces. There is no suggestion to remove
the nutmeg that has been steeped before serving, but it seems a good idea.

To make Meatballs in Head-lettuce.

Take chopped Veal with Veal-fat a little fatter than usual and then spiced with Nutmeg and a little Mace, Pepper, and Salt as appropriate, knead it together, take as many of the tender Heads as you please and clean off the outer leaves and then washed clean and open up the inner leaves of the Head, take then as many Eggs as you have Heads, make also as many little Meatballs and place in the middle of each the yolk of an Egg, put inside the Head, tie with a string, and when the water boils put them in the pot, when it is done you could add to the broth a little finely crushed Rusk and some Butter, some Gooseberries or unripe Grapes or Verjuice, according to everyone's liking.

To make Meatballs still another way.

Take as told above [see "To make Meatballs"] but leave out the Lemon or Orange peels, take a small piece of Bacon cut in an oblong with whole [sprigs of] Parsley [and make] a rather thick [package] which is placed in the middle of the Meatballs, [they] are then cooked and prepared as appropriate, gives good taste; One can also use Veal-fat instead of the Bacon.

To prepare a Joint with Sausages.

Take a Joint, closely lard it, having roasted it with Sausages. One adds in the Butter slices of fresh Lemons, also Cinnamon sticks and crushed cloves and pour it over [the joint]. Is good.

Roasted Hens with a sauce in the French manner.

Take very young Onion, peel even the smallest bulbs, boil in water a little while, pour off the water, add Butter from the dripping pan with some Verjuice or Lemon juice and Pepper with a little Nutmeg stirred together until it comes to a boil and pour it over the Hens.

To stuff a Capon or Hen with Oysters and to roast [them].

Take a good Capon cleaned on the inside then Oysters and some finely crushed Rusk, Pepper, Mace, Nutmeg-powder and a thin little slice or three fresh Lemons,[20] mix together, fill [the bird] with this. When it is roasted one uses for a sauce nothing but the fat from the pan. It is found to be good [that way].

To stew a Duck.

Take a Duck, let it cook with Salt until done, take [some] of the same broth, add to it Butter, Pepper, and Onion cut into slices and some chopped Lovage, let it boil together until the Onion and Herb are done, then add the Bird together with Vinegar and Sugar, let it stew until it is done and just right.

To make a Sauce for a roasted Duck.

Take Mutton broth with Onion boiled together until the Onion has lost its strength, then take out the Onion, then soak toast of White-bread in Wine, rub it through a sieve, in other words the [mutton] broth and the wine with some Vinegar [note: the bread is soaked in all three: broth, wine, and vinegar], add to it Pepper and Cloves, let them boil together, add Sugar as desired and a little Saffron to give color or one can cook a piece of Carrot or Beet-root in it for color. Is good Sauce.

To make a Hare-sauce.

Take a half pint Verjuice, a half dozen Sugar-cookies,[21] let them soak together for half an hour, put into it some whole [misprint *heet* should be

[20]This obviously is a misprint. I believe it should read "thin little slices from three lemons."

[21]In this recipe sugar cookies are used to thicken the sauce, just as nowadays we use ginger snaps to thicken a sauerbraten. Throughout the book, you will find that bread,

heel: whole] cloves, pieces of Cinnamon, a few blades of Mace, a half *loot* crushed Cinnamon, a handful of Sugar or sweet to everyone's liking, a good piece of Butter or Drippings stirred together until it becomes thick. This Sauce is also very good over a roasted Joint larded with Sausages, also without larding as well as over roasted Rabbit.

To make a Sauce for roasted Rabbit.

Take White bread toasted to a nice brown soaked in red Wine with some Vinegar, rub through a Sieve and add Sugar then Butter from the pan, let it boil together. Is good.

To make a Sauce over a roast Hare, Rabbit, Veal-rib, Heart or Beef.

Take a piece of Butter, a half *Roemer* Vinegar, a *Roemer* Rhenish wine, Pepper, Clove-powder, and Sugar, let this boil together until it thickens, then pour it over the roast.

To make a Sauce for a Hare.

Take Sugar or cinnamon cookies with Rhenish wine and Vinegar, add to it Clove-powder, Sugar and a little Mace, let it boil together, then pour it over, is good, otherwise one may take Verjuice.

To [make] a Sauce for a Hare, in another way.

Take a Hare, roast it until it is almost done, then stew it in beef broth until done, then take toasted White-bread and soak it in Mutton broth, rub it through a Sieve with Rhenish wine and Vinegar, then Ginger, Cinnamon, Mace, and Clove-powder, let it cook together with the Drippings, then the Hare with the broth it is stewed in. Is good.

bread crumbs, grated bread, rusk, soaked toasted bread or baked goods, such as *peperkoeck* (see glossary under *koeck*) or cinnamon cookies, are used for thickening, as was the common practice of the period.

To make a Pepper-sauce for roasted Hare, Rabbit or Beef.

Take 4 or 5 slices of Rye bread which has been toasted until black, soak it in Bastert [a very sweet wine], rub it fine, pass it through a hollow cloth [a coarsely woven cloth, such as cheese cloth], and sprinkle some Pepper and crushed Cloves on [it], let it boil together until it is thick enough and then pour it on the Roast.

To make a Sauce for Meat.

Take Mutton broth, Saffron, Ginger, Butter, and Verjuice, let it come to a boil together, add crumbs from White-bread and well-beaten Egg yolks until it is all mixed together and done, pour it over [the meat].

To make Sauce for Meat another way.

Take toasted White-bread, Meat broth, and Vinegar, rub through a Sieve, take Bacon cut fine with Vinegar, well-minced green Herbs, cook it together. It is a good Sauce.

To make *Olipodrigo* which is good.

Take a Hen, a piece of Mutton, a piece of Pork, Veal, put it on the fire in an earthenware pot with water. When it has cooked a little add to the meat and Hen 1 or 2 pigeons, a Teal, and little balls of chopped Veal and Sausages, Sweetbreads, Finches, Endive cooked first, and let it stew merrily, also some Cauliflower as desired, a little Mace and Pepper, stems of Artichokes, Coxcombs. When it is done enough take another little pot and grate breadcrumbs from White-bread into it and a good piece of Butter, 2 or 3 egg yolks, some of the same broth, Lemon juice or Verjuice, place on the fire, only stir until it boils and then stir it into the broth of the *Olipodrigo,* then serve it from the pot.

To make a sumptuous *Olipodrigo.*

Take a clean Capon, Lamb, Veal, Beef, cook it all until almost done, then take Sausages, Pigs' feet, Sheep's feet, and a *krap* [piece of pork with bone in], two Marrow-bones, some little Veal meatballs, cook those together until almost done, Endive cooked for a while, and add Sweetbreads with Ham balls, let it stew together with the Endive in your pot; add whole Pepper and Mace and pieces of Nutmeg, then place the Sheep's and Pigs' feet on the bottom and layer the other meat proportionately, let it stew together for half or three fourth of an hour, then pour off the broth, in the same [broth] add 4 or 5 Egg yolks which have been beaten with some Verjuice, do add some Butter and let it come to a boil together; pour this over everything after you have put it [the meats] in the dish. Also take Chestnuts, Asparagus, or Artichokes, according to the time of the Year, add those (after they are done) to the dish, sprinkle the rim or the entire dish [with] two hard boiled Egg yolks, crushed Rusk, and Parsley which has been cut with the others [the egg yolks and the rusk]. Is good.

To stew a Beef *hutspot* in the Brabant [one of the Seven Provinces] manner.

Take Beef, cook it until almost done then add peeled Ginger cut into slices with Mace, continue to stew until done, take some of the broth, cook it with chopped Parsley and Butter, pour it over [the stew].

To prepare a dish with Veal.

Take Veal minced fine and 6 Eggs stirred together well, with a piece of Butter and chopped Parsley and crushed Cloves; let it cook, then pour Orange juice[22] over [it].

---

[22]This orange juice comes from the bitter and sour Seville oranges, the ones that are used for English marmalade, rather than from the modern sweet variety. To substitute, use the juice of kumquats (sparingly), or if not available a squeeze of lime with a bit of the grated peel.

To stuff a Suckling-pig.

Take the Liver and the Midriff [diaphragm] chopped fine with Parsley and crumbs from White-bread which has been rubbed fine, then Prunes, Currants, Cloves, Nutmeg, Cinnamon. Add the Mutton-broth and Butter in a pot and let it stew dry, stuff the Pig with this [mixture] and roast it (stuck with Cloves) until it is done.

To prepare a Capon in the Spanish way.

Take the Capon, boil it with 3 or 4 pieces of Beef then take whole [blades of] Mace, peeled Ginger, Parsley, Carrots, Rosemary, Saffron, and a piece of Butter, whole Pepper, and a Lemon cut fine, tied together in a cloth, place it together in the broth. When it is stewed together like this take out the cloth with the Lemon, and serve it.

To make a *Hutspot* from a Capon.

Take a Capon, chop it into pieces, cook in water until well-done, take then crumbs of White-bread, Cinnamon, Ginger, Saffron, Sugar, and Marrow from Marrow-bones with some Dates from which the stones have been removed and slices of a Lemon. Let it stew for half an hour in a flat [shallow earthenware] pot. Is good.

To stew a Hen.

Take a Hen, let it cook until very well done, then soak toasted Bread in your broth and mash fine, then add Nutmeg, Cloves, Ginger in your broth with a part Rhenish wine and some Sugar, let it stew together for half an hour.

To stuff a young Hen.

Take a grated White-bread, and 3 hard-boiled Egg yolks which have been mashed fine, with some smoked Bacon, and smoked Meat, do

17. *Still Life with Réchaud and Glass Decanter,* Willem Kalf. This still life clearly explains how food is "stewed between two platters." Note the réchaud and the nutmeg grater, which look very similar to their modern counterparts. Courtesy private Canadian collection, used by permission.

chop it fine, then crushed Mace, Pepper, Ginger, and a little Saffron; all well stirred together, the Hen is stuffed with this [mixture], then stewed with Butter, Wine, Water. When done some Verjuice and Saffron is added to the Broth, then it is served.

To make a Hash.

Take a cold Roast, either Mutton or Veal, Hens, Capons, Turkeys, Etc., cut it to your liking, add to it Verjuice, Lemon-juice, or Vinegar, whatever you have, with some Water, furthermore Pepper, Mace, and Butter and stew it between 2 platters.

To make a chopped Hash.

Take Veal or Mutton, boiled or roasted, chop it into small pieces, add to it slices of Lemons, Pepper, and Nutmeg, Mutton-broth, Verjuice, and some Butter, and let it stew together this way.

To stew Rabbits.

Wash the Rabbits, tie them with the head between the legs, then take two small bowls of water, a small bowl of Vinegar, a little crushed Pepper, Cloves, and Nutmeg and put them on to stew. Some also add Onions. Then take a crushed Rusk or grated White-bread to thicken the broth. At the last moment add a good piece of Butter.

Rabbits in another way.

Boil the Rabbits whole in clean water with some Salt, skim them clean, carve them and fry them in some Butter in the pan until they turn red [reddish brown], then add a sauce of Butter and some Vinegar and Sugar. Stir this together in the pan so that it becomes a thick little sauce and pour it then over the Rabbits. It tastes all right.

To prepare an Ox-tongue.

Take a Tongue, first cut in half and then cut into 3 or 4 pieces. Stew with some Broth, red Wine, Butter, Cloves, Pepper, Ginger, Cinnamon, Sugar, and some Vinegar until it is done enough. Is good.

To stew the whole haunch of Mutton with Horseradish.

Take two handfuls of grated Horseradish, 4 or 5 spoons grated White-bread, mix these together with Meat-broth and Vinegar [make it] as thick as stewed Apples, add to it Butter and Sugar, let it then stew together until it is as thick as appropriate, but let the Meat cook separately in another pot, place the Horseradish-sauce in the dish first and place the Meat on top.

To stew a *Hutspot* of everything.

Take a Capon, Mutton, Beef, and Pork, a Duck or Widgeon, and Sausages, put this all together in a pot over the fire, appropriately salted and skimmed clean, and cooked until well done, then stew it with some weak broth with some Ginger and Pepper and add to it Savoy cabbage which has been cooked first and let it stew together.

To stew Calf's-feet.

Take Mutton broth, Ginger, Verjuice, Saffron, Parsley chopped fine, a good piece of Butter, let it stew together this way.

To make a Sauce for *Patrijsen* or *Veldhoenders* [both are partridges].

Take hard-boiled Egg yolks, crumbs from a White-bread, mash it all very fine, then [add] Sugar, Saffron, and white Onions, bring it to a boil in Mutton-broth, pour it on your Roast.

The same in a different manner.

Take a slice of Wheat-bread, fry it, and then grate it [add] a half *pint* Verjuice and some crushed Pepper and whole Mace, add to it one or two spoons of Drippings, stir it until it is cooked enough, pour it on the Roast. This Sauce is also good over boiled Artichokes.

To make a proper Sauce.

Take the crumbs of White-bread and finely crushed Almonds, Verjuice, Sugar, and some Ginger. Cook this all together thoroughly. Is a good Sauce.

To remove the rank taste from a Goose.

Take a Goose which has been washed very clean, place a yellow Carrot inside it, let it boil for one or two hours, remove the Carrot and stuff it [the goose] as you desire, place that [the goose] on the Spit and let it roast until done. You will not taste any rankness.

To stuff a roasted Goose or Duck.

Take out all the loose fat inside the Goose, take a Wheat-bread of 2 *stuyvers*,[23] cut off the crusts, finely grate them, mix in a half *pond* Currants, one and a half *loot* Cinnamon, two heaping spoons of Sugar, a good piece of Butter with a little Rhenish wine but as dry as possible just so it has been moistened. It will be a good stuffing. Geese and Ducks are stuffed also with Chestnuts from which the peels and membranes have been removed [and which have been mixed] with Butter.

To fry Calf's ears.[24]

Take chopped Veal which is done, add to it Nutmeg, Mace, Sugar, and 2 or 3 Egg yolks, stir together, then take sliced White-bread and place the above on the bread and fry it like this together in a pan in the Butter.

About All Sorts of Fish.

To roast a piece of Sturgeon.

Remove the fin and the scales, stick it with Cloves, let it roast; baste it well with Butter, when it is done take it from the spit, place it in a pot, then do stew it with Rhenish wine, Vinegar, Cinnamon, and Nutmeg. When dished up like this it is good.

[23]The *stuyver* is a coin now worth one-twentieth of a guilder. We know from ordinances in the Netherlands as well as in New Netherland that periodically the price and weight of bread were determined by the authorities. A wheat bread of "two *stuyvers*" indicated a bread of a certain weight. In the case of "a *stuyver* Rosewater," which we find in a later recipe, it indicates a measure of the flavoring that could be obtained for that price at that time.

[24]These are not ears at all but bread slices topped with a well-seasoned veal mixture.

18. *The Fish Woman,* Adriaen van Ostade. A wide variety of fish was eaten in the seventeenth century, as we can learn from the recipes. The fish seller is showing off her codfish. On the table are also some flounder and a rock crab. An enticing piece of salmon appears in the background. Courtesy Rijksmuseum-Stichting, Amsterdam.

To roast a Bream on the spit.

Take a Bream with roe after it has been cleaned, cut open the belly and take out only the roe, chop it with Egg yolks, Parsley, Nutmeg, Mace, Pepper, and Butter, then place it back inside and sew up the Bream. After it is roasted take the Butter from the pan, add 2 or 3 Anchovies, some Verjuice, bring it to a boil and cook until the Anchovies are melted. When dishing up sprinkle the rim of your platter with Oregano.

To roast the tail of a Pike on the spit.

Take Anchovies or Salted Herring, lard the Tail with them, roast it on the Spit in this way until done. The Sauce is Butter from the pan, Anchovies or fine pieces of Herring brought to a boil with Verjuice or Lemon juice. In this way one also roasts the Tail of a Codfish.

To boil a Pike in the Spanish manner.

Take a Lemon, cut it in slices, place them in a little pot with some Rhenish wine, Water, Butter, Ginger, Saffron, and Cloves, let it stew together until it is [done] enough, then pour it on a platter and place the boiled Pike in it.

To boil a Pike or Carp [until] blue.

Take a Carp or Pike, cut him through, pour Vinegar on it, when the water with Salt boils place the Pike in it and cook it very hard. It will be blue. In this manner you can also cook a Carp and to have it completely blue some cook it in half Water and half Rhenish wine.

To prepare a Pike differently in the French manner.

Take a Pike cooked in water with some Vinegar and salted appropriately, then cut Bacon in cubes and fry it in Butter until it is red [reddish brown], place it in a pot, add to it some Broth, Rhenish wine, Vinegar, Mace, Pepper, and Ginger. Let it boil until properly thickened, place the Pike in that [sauce] and dish up this way.

To stew Salmon in a different manner.

Remove the scales of the Salmon, wash it clean, take a little tin bowl of water and a little bowl of Wine-vinegar for each slice of Salmon, grate a piece of Wheat-bread and some whole Pepper, half a Nutmeg, a little crushed Mace, no Salt. Place these in a flat [shallow earthenware] pot, let it stew together, add a little Butter to it after it has stewed a while.

To stew a Carp in the High-german manner.

Take a Carp well cleaned. Do save that blood. Split and cut into pieces, then add the blood in a pot with a *pint* of Rhenish wine and some Vinegar and Water, round slices of Onion. Do fry those first in the Butter, then add to the Carp some Cloves, Mace, Nutmeg, Saffron and a good piece of Butter. Let it stew together. *Probatum est* [It has been approved].

To stew Codfish.

Take the thick slices of fish, place them in a tin platter not quite covered with water, sprinkle some crushed Pepper over it and whole Mace, a little Salt, and some crushed Rusk, and do add Butter. Let it stew together about an hour and a half with fire under it and above, then add a fresh Lemon or Lemon-juice. It is quite easy to eat. In this manner one can also stew Sea Flounder, Tench and Roach and a Tail of Haddock, also Eel.

To stew small Bundles of Young Eel with Herbs.[25]

Split the Eel open and wash clean. Take Sorrel, Chervil, and Parsley, some Rice, a little Mace, tied to close [and] boiled in water, some Salt in it. When the Eel floats then take it out and place on an earthenware colander and a sauce of Butter and Vinegar with an Egg is poured over it. Is good.

To stew an Eel.

Take an Eel washed clean and cut into pieces, add to it water, Butter, Ginger, Onion, little Salt. Let it stew together until it is [done] enough, then add chopped Parsley and Lovage to the pot, continue to cook for a little while and dish him up.

[25]Sewel's dictionary gives the meaning of *Bond-ael* as "bundles of eels stuffed with herbs." Furthermore, "ael" means "young eel." I speculate that the word *bundles* refers to the way young eels are sold — in bundles — rather than the way they are cooked. When you make this recipe, tie each eel separately to close, but leave room for the rice to swell in cooking.

To make a *Hutspot* from Sturgeon.

Take Sturgeon, cook it and drain it, then cook until done and well salted: take some of the broth with Rhenish wine, Ginger and Sugar, some Vinegar, Nutmeg and Mace and when that is boiled together is a good Sauce.

To make a Sauce for a Boiled Sturgeon.

Take young Onion cooked in Butter, Chervil, Parsley, Pepper, and Wine-vinegar, let it cook together. It is a good Sauce.

To prepare a salted Salmon.

Take slices as thick as a finger, soak them in Rain-water for 18 hours, refresh the water in between, [place] clean rain water [in a pot] hung over [the fire] and let it boil; then add the Salmon and skim well. When it has come to a boil it is enough because when it is cooked [for a] long [time] it loses its fattiness; one eats it with Vinegar or with Butter and Vinegar cooked together.

To boil Lobster or Crab.

Take Water, Vinegar, Salt and Pepper-powder, let it cook well together [let it come to a rolling boil], add the Lobster or Crab. He will have beautiful color.

To make a good dish of Crabs or Lobsters.

Remove (after they have been cooked until done) all the dirt from the Crab or Lobsters, add to it Parsley cut fine, Pepper, Mace, Nutmeg, and Butter. Stir it together until it is done. At that moment Lemon-juice or Verjuice is added; when it is a Crab it is generally stirred or stewed in its own shell.

To stew Oysters or Mussels.

Take Oysters or Mussels (but the Mussels have to be alive when taken from the Shell), place them in a Dish, place them on a Chafing Dish; if the Mussels were cooked first add some Water and Vinegar or Verjuice, otherwise do not. Then do add Butter and Mace and let it stew until it is done, then add some Lemon-juice and finely crushed Rusk.

To fry Mussels in the Pan.

Take Mussels, take them from the Shell while alive, place them on an earthenware colander so that the juices drain off, then roll in Wheat-flour with some Salt, fried in Oil or Butter and eaten with some Verjuice is good to those who like them.

About All Sorts of Baked and Cooked [Items], etc.

To make a tasty *Kandeel* [drink].[26]

Take a *pint* of water and a *pint* of Rhenish wine, beat 6 Eggs without the Cicatricle [membranous thread] very well, stir them together, place it on the fire until it comes to a boil. Do add to it Sugar, Mace, Nutmeg, Cinnamon, and Cloves. It is good to drink; some use it as a sauce over a stewed Hen, some also toast White-bread in it to eat [the toast is floated on top], some add Butter to it.

To make a Custard.[27]

Take a pint of sweet Milk, let it come to a boil, stir it until it is almost cold, then take 8 Eggs from which the Cicatricle has been removed and

[26] *Kandeel*, a spiced drink like eggnog but made with wine, was a favorite potion for celebrations, particularly the birth of a child. I think the recipe tastes much better with less or no water. Nowadays it is made with egg yolks only, rather than with whole eggs. The seasoning is fairly typical; although modern recipes sometimes omit the mace, I like to use it (see my adaptation).

[27] The Dutch words *vla*, *vlade*, or *vlaay* all have a dual meaning of custard, or thin porridge, and a round, flat pie. The recipes represented here are more custards than pies,

which have been well beaten, with a half *mutsjen* Rosewater, [28] two spoons of Sugar, and stir that into the Milk in a dish or Custard-pan,[29] place it on a slow fire, but on the lid a little more fire and let it stand until it is stiff, but it should not boil.

To make an Apple-Custard.

Take *Guldelingen* [a sweet, gold-colored eating apple] peeled and cut into pieces, place them in a pot with Water, Rhenish wine and Butter, thus let them simmer together, do mash them into pieces, then add to it half as much White-bread, 5 Egg yolks, Ginger, and Sugar all mixed together. It is good.

The same Thing but different.

Take sour Apples cut into slices, fried in the pan. When they are done take the crumbs of 2 White-breads and soak those in a little bowl of Buttermilk, and then mashed fine, take 6 Eggs, 2 spoons of Sugar mixed together. Pour this on the Apples and cover them, place fire on the lid, and also fire under the dish. Is good.

although they might have had a crust. Anna de Peyster has a similar recipe in her manuscript for an apple-custard, for which she uses a puff paste crust.

[28]Rosewater, distilled water made from rose petals, was used as a flavoring as frequently as we now use vanilla. According to Hess it was not until the early nineteenth century that vanilla replaced rosewater in our preference. (Hess, 267.)

[29]I believe that "custard-pan" means an earthenware dish shaped more or less like a modern deep-dish pie plate. The cooking method—with fire on top of "the lid," seems to suggest it has a matching lid. If not, a lid surely could be borrowed from another pan. Plates or shallow dishes were also used as lids. It sounds rather tricky to make custard on direct heat, but if the fire is slow enough, it can be done. Another method of baking a custard might have been to place it in a *taert* pan or simply to place it in the oven after the bread had been removed.

To make an Apple custard in another manner.[30]

Take Apples, *Peper-koeck,* Water, Ginger, Pepper, Cinnamon and Cloves and for each pot of Milk that you add also add 14 Eggs and for each pot of Water add a Nutmeg, Sugar, and Eggs. That way you can make them as large or small as you desire.

To make a lovely Apple-a-Milk.

Take *Aeghten* [a certain kind of sour apple] Apples peeled and with the cores well removed, place them in a pot with some Butter and Rosewater, let it cook until it is fine like porridge, mash it steadily with the spoon, then add a little Wheat-flour, add a proportionate amount of Buttermilk, let it cook together until it is like sweet cream, then add some Sugar and White-bread.

To make an Apple-porridge [a batter for a kind of pancake].

Take Loaf-Sugar, crush Rusk into it, add 4 beaten Eggs so that it is thick, grated Wheat-bread. Place this in a frying pan with Butter that is somewhat short [meaning: not too much butter] add to it that Apple porridge [thick applesauce, presumably made ahead of time] and then let it fry like any other *koek,* covered with a dish.

To make a Custard of Lemons.

Take the juice from the Lemons and the yolks of 8 Eggs, but add only the white of 4, grate a White-bread of half a *stuyver,* then [add] a *pint* of sweet Milk and Sugar proportionately, neither too vigorously nor too slow you should let it boil.

[30]This is one of the few unclear recipes in the book. I believe that the author means to say that for every pot of milk 14 eggs are added; and for each pot of water used to boil the mixture of apples, *peper-koeck,* and spices, as well as a nutmeg should be added. But why eggs are repeated I do not know. It seems that the recipe makes a porridge, but the phrase "then you can make them as large or as small" seems to point to some sort of pancake.

To make Spanish Porridge.

Take a half *pond* of Rice-flour, a half *pond* Loaf-sugar crushed, a *mengele* of sweet Milk, a *mutsje* Rosewater, stir it well so that it [the mixture] is smooth and there are no lumps. Place it on the fire and stir it steadily, let it boil so long that it becomes stiff, then serve it in dishes. It tastes very good.

To make Cream-porridge.

Take 12 Egg yolks, a *pint* of cream, pour the Eggs through a sieve and mix well with the Cream, add to it Rosewater and Sugar appropriately, place it on the fire, stir it gently until it thickens, but do not boil or it would separate.

To make Cream from Rice.

Take a *mengelen* of Cream, 2 handfuls of Rice Flour, white Sugar and Wheat-flour of each 8 *loot,* an Egg yolk beaten in Rosewater. Stir this well together with the afore-mentioned Cream and place it on a coal fire stirring steadily so that it becomes as thick as Water-porridge.

To fry Rice *koecxkens*
[fritters the size and shape of cookies].

Boil Rice in sweet Milk until very thick [but] so that the kernels stay whole, cool it, add then some Saffron, a little Cinnamon with crushed Rusk which has been soaked in Rosewater, and Sugar and eight or ten Eggs and Rosewater proportionately, then stir in the Rice and then fry in Butter and grate Sugar over it.

To fry Rice *koecxkens* another way.

Take a quarter *pond* of Rice cooked until half done, 3 Rusks, 4 Eggs, a quarter *pond* of Currants, Sugar, and Cinnamon Sticks with Rosewater, stir together. Make fritters [the shape and size of cookies] from it, fry in the pan, ample Butter. Are good.

To fry *Deuse Geertjes* [sweet Geertjes — a girl's name].

Take 4 stale round White-breads finely grated, add an Egg for each Bread, mix it with sweet Cream, add Rosewater to it, Cinnamon and Sugar, a small cup of melted Butter. Stir this together then quickly fry them in Butter because otherwise they would fall.

To fry green Leaves.

Take young leaves of Bugloss, Borage, or Clary and break off the stem, take out the ribs from the middle of the leaf without breaking that [the leaf], wash the leaves and put them down to drain dry, place beaten Eggs in a flat dish and dip the leaves in it and fit two leaves together, the backs on the outside, then fry in Butter and grate Sugar over them.

To make Egg-fritters which are good.

Take all sorts of herbs as for [the dish] Pot Herbs [see recipe entitled "To Cook Pot-Herbs"] and some Fennel, Dill, Rocket, Chervil, Violet leaves, Tansy, Watercress, Sorrel, Betony, Hepatica, Chicory, Spinach and the leaves of black Currants, some Leeks, Calendula, *madelief-kruydt [Bellis perennis]*, cut them fine together and mix them with Eggs and finely crushed Rusk. When they are fried they are quite tasty.

To bake an Apple [egg]fritter.

Take 12 *Kabau* [type of apple] apples, cut them in pieces as you would for a *Taert*, place them with a good piece of Butter in a flat [shallow earthenware] pot and some Sugar, shake [the pot] often but do not stir when they start to get done, mix in 4 to 6 beaten Eggs then take a pan with Butter and when the Butter starts to fry sprinkle a thick [layer] of finely crushed Rusk on it to cover the bottom of the pan, mixed with Sugar and Cinnamon, place the Apples on top; then sprinkle again with the afore-mentioned Rusk until the Apples are covered, place a little fire on the lid and let it bake this way.

To fry a Bacon [egg]fritter.

Place thin pieces of Bacon in the pan, soak 2 or 3 stale White-breads with the crusts cut off in sweet Milk, when it is saturated mash it fine in a flat [shallow earthenware] pot, stir in 6 to 8 Eggs, pour [the mixture] onto the Bacon and fry.

To fry Groeninger [from the town or province of Groningen] Pancakes.

Take a *pond* of Wheat-flour, 3 Eggs, a quarter *pond* of Currants and Some Cinnamon, this [mixture] is fried in Butter.[31] Is good.

To fry common Pancakes.

For each *pond* of Wheat-flour take a *pint* of sweet Milk and 3 Eggs. Some add some Sugar to it.

To fry the best kind of Pancakes.

Take 5 or 6 Eggs beaten with clean, running water, add to it Cloves, Cinnamon, Mace, and Nutmeg with some Salt, beat it with some Wheat-flour as thick as you like, fry them and sprinkle them with Sugar; these are prepared with running water because [when prepared] with Milk or Cream they would be tough.

To fry Waffles.

For each *pond* of Wheat-flour take a *pint* of sweet Milk, a little tin bowl of melted Butter with 3 or 4 Eggs, a spoonful of Yeast well stirred together.

[31]"Butterfat," the translation of the word *botervet* in the text, is the fatty part of milk from which butter is made. It cannot be used until it is made into butter, and it is even better for frying when made into clarified butter. Use either one when you try this recipe.

19. *Pancake Maker,* follower of Nicolaes Maes. Everybody loves pancakes. They are a simple, yet filling meal. A barrel makes a hearthside table and holds a pitcher and a large lump of butter. Courtesy Museum of Fine Arts, Boston, Seth K. Sweetser Fund.

To fry Wafers.

Take a *pond* Wheat-flour, a *loot* Cinnamon, a half *loot* Ginger, 2 Eggs, a half beer glass Rhenish-wine , a *stuyver* Rosewater, a small bowl Butter without Salt, a little Sugar; beaten with some lukewarm water until the thickness of Pancake [batter] and fried in the iron. Is delicious.

To fry *Olie-koecken.*

For 2 *pond* of Wheat-flour take 2 *pond* long Raisins, when they have been washed clean soak them in lukewarm water, a cup of the best Apples, peel them and cut them in very small pieces without the cores, a quarter *pond* or one and a half [quarter *pond:* 6 ounces] peeled Almonds, a *loot* Cinnamon, a quarter *loot* white Ginger, a few Cloves this crushed together, half a small bowl of melted Butter, a large spoon Yeast, and not quite a *pint* of lukewarm sweet Milk, because it must be a thick batter [so thick] that the batter is tough when spooned and then everything stirred together. Let it rise then take a *mengelen* of the best Rapeseed [Colza] oil, add a crust of Bread, a half Apple. Place it on the fire and let it burn, keep turning the bread and Apple until it blackens and hardens, then pour in a dash of clean water, let it cool in the air, then put it back on the fire when you want to use it.[32]

To fry *koecxkens* [fritters in the shape and size of cookies] from Eggs, or Puff-bread.

Take a Bread that is about 3 or 4 days old, grate it very fine, then soak it in sweet Milk until it is thick and has absorbed the liquid, then take some Rosewater and Sugar and 6 or more Eggs according to how much Bread you have (some take also some Currants and Cinnamon with it) and then fry in Butter. Everyone [can make them] as big as he desires.

[32]Adding a crust of bread and a half apple to the rapeseed oil is apparently a method to clear or clean the oil and remove disagreeable odors. The apple alone must cause the oil to splatter, but then, to make it worse, water is added. Fortunately, we can use other cooking oils; and the recipe itself for the *olie-koecken* is a treasure.

To bake a Pudding which is delicious.

Take 13 large Rusks crushed fine, a half *pond* Veal-suet cut into cubes, place in a flat pot, grate into it a Nutmeg, half a spoon of Ginger, a little Salt, and stir this together and mix it very dry with warm sweet Milk in which the Veal-suet first has been warmed; add to that half *pond* Currants, 10 Eggs, an ample quarter of a *pond* of Wheat-flour, half a tin spoonful of Yeast, grease the pan with cold Butter and let it rise in the warm pan for about an hour, and then bake it.

To boil a Pudding which is uncommonly good.

Take a *pond* and [a] half of Wheat-flour, three quarter *pond* of Currants washed clean, a half *pond* Kidney-suet, cut it very small, 3 Eggs, one and a half Nutmegs, grated fine, a little Salt, mix it with a little sweet Milk so dry that one kneads it like a Bread and tie it in a clean cloth rather close and throw it into a pot with boiling water and let it boil for two hours, then it is done.

About All Sorts of Taerten.

To make Dough for *Taerten.*

Take Wheat-flour, Butter, Rosewater, Sugar and a few Eggs each as appropriate.

To make a Dough crust without Butter.

Take a quarter *pond* fine Wheat flour, place it in an earthenware Pot, bake it in the Oven with the Bread, then make a dough with the yolks of 2 or 3 Eggs and a *pint* of Cream, mix with an eighth of a *pond* finely crushed Loaf-sugar, and this way you will make a short [crust] Dough without Butter or Fat.

To make an Almond-*taert*.

Take a half *pond* peeled Almonds, a quarter *pond* Sugar, 3 whole Eggs with the whites and 3 more Egg yolks, an eighth of a *pond* of sweet Butter, Rosewater as much as necessary to crush the Almonds[33]: first thoroughly sprinkle the [baking] sheet that you are using with Wheat-flour.

To make a Pear-*taert*.

Take 12 of the tastiest, peeled Pears, Currants, and Sugar of each a quarter *pond*, 6 *loot* Butter, Ginger, Cinnamon of each a half *loot* in a crust as described before.

To make an Apple-*taert*.

Take of the best Apples, peel them and cut them in quarters, remove the cores, cook them with Rhenish wine in an earthenware pot until they thicken, add to them a good piece of Sugar, crushed Cinnamon, powder of Sandalwood, Rosewater, rub it all together with a wooden spoon through a sieve set up side down,[34] place it in the crust and bake it in the Oven. It will be good.

Another way to bake an Apple-*taert*.

Take a *pond* of Flour, 4 spoons water with 2 or 3 spoons Sugar, this [water and sugar] cooked together into a Syrup, add to it an Egg, furthermore as much Butter as is needed to make a suitable Dough, this gives

---

[33]Making almond paste in a mortar with a pestle is a tedious and time-consuming task. The addition of rosewater is necessary to prevent the paste from becoming oily.

[34]A seventeenth-century sieve was not domed but a large, rather shallow drum-shaped utensil. The sides were of shaped splint wood, and cloth of various degrees of fineness of weave was stretched tight on one side. For sifting flour you hold the sieve "right side up," place the flour inside, and shake it over a large dish; for pureeing, and so forth, you place it "upside down" over a shallow basin, so that the sides of the sieve sit firmly on the table.

a good crust: Then one takes 20 or 25 good Apples according to their size, peeled and cut into small pieces, place them in an earthenware pot, add Butter to it, place it on the fire and shake [the pot] often until they are cooked down, then place them in your crust to cover the Bottom, then [layer] again Sugar, Currants, and Butter, then again Apples until your crust is filled, and then placed on the fire.

To make an Apple-*taert* in yet another way.

Take Apples, peel them and cut them in quarters and remove the cores, and then cut them in even smaller thin slivers, three quarter *pond* Currants washed clean and three quarter *pond* Sugar, a *loot* crushed Cinnamon, then place the Dough in the pan and first sprinkle Apples into it, then Currants, Sugar, and Cinnamon and pieces of Butter. Repeat the layers until the pan is full; some add crushed Anise-seed. Then a lid of Dough on top, cut a hole in the lid here and there and let it bake with fire underneath and on top.

To make an Apple-*taert* in the Walloon manner.

Take peeled Apples with the cores removed, boil them in Rhenish wine until well done, add Butter to them, Ginger, Sugar, Currant, Cinnamon cooked all together very well, then stir the yolks of 2 Eggs, place [the mixture] in your Dough and bake in the Oven as mentioned before.

To make a Cherry *taert*.

Take the most beautiful Cherries and when you have made the crust sprinkle enough Sugar on the bottom to cover it, place a layer of Cherries on it and then again a layer of Sugar until the crust is filled, not forgetting Cinnamon, cover it and let it bake until done. In the same manner you can also make a *taert* of Gooseberries, Currants, Strawberries, *Barbarisse* Plums [a type of plum], and all soft fruits.

Cherry-*taert* in another manner.

Take two and a half *pond* of Cherries, remove the pits over a flat pot (so that the juice is not lost), 3 Rusks crushed, three quarter *pond* Sugar, a *loot* crushed Cinnamon, stir this together and place it then in the Dough in the *Taert-pan*[35] and little pieces of Butter on top, cover it with a lid of Dough in which there are here and there only small holes, otherwise the juice will run out.

To make a Chervil-*taert*.

Take Chervil cut the first time [in the season] and cut it fine, press the juice out of it then mix with Butter, Currants, Sugar, crushed Rusks, Cinnamon and Rosewater with 6 or 8 Eggs and then placed in the crust and baked.

Chervil-*taert* in another manner.

Take young Chervil cut the first time [in the season] pick it over, wash it, cut it fine, add to it half a *pond* of Currants, 6, 7, or 8 Eggs, then take a half *pint* of sweet Milk and a stale White-bread of a *stuyver*, cut off the crusts and grate it fine, place it in the Milk and boil it until it is a thick porridge. A good piece of Butter needs to be added to the porridge while it is cooking and stir this into the Chervil, then Sugar with some melted Butter and if it is too thin crush into it a Rusk or two, place it in the Dough in the pan and sprinkle it with crushed Cinnamon, then make a lattice top for it and let it bake with fire below and on top and when this is served at the table grate Loaf-sugar over it.

[35]Van 't Veer explains that a *taert-pan* is a "large copper pan ... usually oval, not too great in height in proportion to the large surface" (Annie Van 't Veer, *Oud-Hollands Kookboek*, 148).

To make a Pinched Apple-*taert*.[36]

Take Apples cut fine and add Egg yolks, Cinnamon, and Sugar and melted Butter, mix it together, place it in the Dough and let it bake.

To make a Meat-*taert*.

Take boiled Beef, Mutton, or Veal, fry it in some Kidney-suet until very done, add to it Egg yolks, Ginger, Cinnamon-powder, Salt, and Sugar, bake it in your crust. It is good.

To make a Marrow-*taert*.

Take Marrow from the bones and very fine white sugar, Cinnamon-powder, and Ginger, with chopped Veal and Currants. Mix this together thoroughly, bake [misprint *hackt* means chop; should be *backt:* bake] then in Dough. It is agreeable.

To make a Lemon-*taert*.

Take the grated outer yellow of 4 Lemons and [mix] it with 6 sour Apples and 6 Egg yolks, half of the crumbs from a White-bread of half *stuyver,* a little Butter and finely grated Sugar and bake it.

To bake a *Sucade-taert*.[37]

Take [the marrow from] 2 Marrow-bones, 3 or 4 Sweetbreads, 6 [hard-cooked] Egg yolks and that chopped together, also a half *pond Sucade* cut fine, Sugar, Pine Nuts, Rosewater and 3 Eggs stirred together, some Spanish Wine is poured on, some Cinnamon, Cloves, Ginger [are added] then placed in the crust and baked for a half hour.

[36]According to Johanna Maria van Winter the word *doornepen* in the original text is a bastardization of the word *Doornick*. This recipe for an apple taert as made in the town of Doornick already appears in medieval cookbooks.

[37] *Sucade, succade,* or *succats* all mean candied peel. Although this is usually citron, it can be made from many fruits, such as cherries, orange or lemon, or the candied stem of Angelica. Anna de Peyster refers to "green citron" in her recipe for almond tarts, by which she meant, I believe, Angelica.

To make a Cream-*taert*.

Take a *pint* of sweet Cream, 4 Egg yolks beaten with Rosewater and some Wheat-flour to make it somewhat thick, cook this in the pan on coals stirring constantly so that it does not burn. When it has come to a boil add Sugar to it and continue to boil until it is done. Pour it in your Dough and let it bake.

To make a *taert* of small Cheeses.

Take little fresh Cream cheeses and Egg yolks with Wheat-flour and Butter, make a dough[-like filling] from it, place it in your crust. It is good.

To bake an Apricot-*taert*.

Take Apricots, peel them and place them in the *Taert* then top with some Cinnamon, Sugar, *Sucade* and some Butter and bake a half hour.

To make a Plum-*taert*.

Take Plums, cook them until done, rub through a Sieve, dress them with Egg yolks, Sugar, and Cinnamon, Cloves and melted Butter, place them in your crust, bake it without upper crust then sprinkle with Cinnamon.

To make a Spinach-*taert* the color green.

Take Spinach, cook it in Rhenish wine until it is mush, rub it through a Sieve as thickly as you can, add Rosewater, a lot of Sugar and Cinnamon, and cook it until it is as thick as Marmalade. When it is cool place it then in Dough as described before and it will be green and tasty.

To bake a Shoe-makers *Taert*.

Take sour Apples, peel them and cut them in pieces and when they have been cooked until done mash them fine, then take Butter, Sugar, and Currants, everyone according to his taste, and stir that together with 4 or 5 Eggs, then take grated Wheat bread and place that on the bottom of a platter, place your Apples on top and again grate Wheat-bread on top [of the apples], cover it with a lid from a *Taert-pan* place fire on it. It makes a good crust.

To make a *Taert* from Calf's-tongue.

Take a Calf's-tongue cooked until done and cleaned so that it does not look like Tongue, chop it fine with 12 peeled sour Apples without cores, add to it crushed Rusk, three-quarter *pond* Currants, a Nutmeg, Ginger, and Cinnamon with a little Sugar then place it in your crust and you will find it delicious.

To make a *Taert* from Calf's-feet.

Take Calf's-feet that are well-done, chop them very fine together with hard-cooked Egg yolks, dress them with Cinnamon, Ginger, Currants, Sugar and melted Butter all stirred together with Rhenish wine, *Sucade* and Pine Nuts, and then baked for half an hour.

About All Sorts of Pasteyen *with Their Sauces.*

To make a Beef-*pastey.*

Take Beef which has been placed in hot water for a while, then place into Wine-vinegar for a night, then well larded with Bacon, rolled in Salt and Pepper and then placed in the Dough and baked; For 3 *pond* of Meat one takes a *loot* Pepper, one and a half *loot* Ginger and one and a half *loot* Nutmegs, a quarter *loot* Cloves and Vinegar as appropriate. Some also take a little Saffron.

To make a sour Lemon-*pastey.*

Take Veal and Veal-suet and a fresh Lemon with it, chop it fine together, then spice it with Salt, Mace, Pepper and Nutmeg, also 2 or 3 Egg yolks, stir together, place in the crust with slices of Lemon on top and a lot of Butter, bake it for an hour; the sauce should be Mutton-broth, Egg yolks, Verjuice and Butter brought to a boil together.

To make a Hen-*pastey.*

Take Hens, boil them for a while, crack the bones and place them in the *Pastey* then spiced with Mace, Pepper, Nutmeg. Top them with Sausages, Sweetbreads, little meatballs made from chopped Veal, Coxcombs, Artichoke bottoms, Asparagus, Chestnuts, and especially Butter and then bake for an hour and a half; you will make the sauce with Mutton-broth and Verjuice with two beaten Egg yolks and Butter. Let this come to a boil together.

To make a Spring Chicken-*pastey.*

Take the Spring Chickens washed clean, the Legs, Breast, and Bones cracked, place them in a crust made from the best Dough, place them together, be sure to add Butter and then fill it with Coxcombs, Artichokes, Sheep's-feet, Sausages, Sweetbreads, and whatever else is tasty, then some Mace, Pepper, Nutmeg, Salt, cover with Butter, pour over it some Rosewater and sprinkle with Sugar and some Verjuice, as much as you think is enough, also 1 or 2 Egg yolks, cover with the crust and thus let it bake in the Oven.

To make a sweet Spring Chicken-*pastey.*

Take the Spring Chicken boiled a little while, place it in the *Pastey,* spice it with Cinnamon, Cloves, a little Nutmeg, and Ginger, place with it Damson Prunes, candied Pears and Cherries, *Sucade,* Pine Nuts and Butter; let it bake for an hour. The sauce should be made with Wine and Sugar. Or otherwise sweet Cream heated with Egg yolks and Sugar, then it is also called a sweet Cream *pastey.*

To make a Finch-*pastey.*

Take Finches, wash them very well and boil them a little [while] then place them in the *Pastey,* dress them with Cinnamon, Sugar, Currants, Pine Nuts, *Sucade* and Butter and bake this all together for half an hour: the sauce should be Rhenish wine and Sugar.

To make a tasty Pot-*pastey.*

Take 2 *pond* of Beef or Veal, when it has been cooked and chopped fine a *pond* of Currants, some crushed Cloves and Nutmeg, a little Ginger and Cinnamon, and mix with the Meat-broth a half *pint* of Rhenish wine and small pieces of dried Orange-peel which have been reconstituted and boiled in small Beer and some Pine Nuts, a good piece of Butter, a half *pond* of Prunes, Sugar; but if you want to save the Pot-*pastey* for some time you should not first add the Prunes [implying that they can be added later].

20. *The Pig on the Ladder*, Michiel van Musscher. A traditional way of hanging a slaughtered animal. The children are blowing up the bladder to use as a ball or balloon. A vegetable woman comes by with her wheelbarrow full of garden-fresh produce. Courtesy Amsterdams Historisch Museum, Amsterdam.

THE DUTCH BUTCHERING TIME.[38]

*Instructing, how one shall supply oneself
with a stock of Meat against the Winter.*

The preparation of the Tub.

The tub or the meat-vat in which one places the salted Meat needs to be properly prepared and closed and left overnight filled with Water to swell. Pour [the cold water] out and pour in boiling hot water in which you have boiled Vine-leaves, cover the tub and let it get heated [through] until the water is almost cold; then pour it out. In a pipkin with fire sprinkle a handful of Cloves, but not all at the same time, turn the tub over onto [the pipkin], let it stand to smoke out, after that one can pour melted candle wax along the grooves of the inside bottom and this happens because brine is very apt to penetrate. Before one places the Meat in the tub the bottom is sprinkled with Salt.

About salting the Meat.

The usual way of salting is to rub the Meat very well with salt all around on all sides and in all corners and then to pack it in the tub and sprinkle salt between [layers] packed as tightly as possible. But here is another way: Make brine so strong that no more salt will melt in it but an Egg will float in it, salt the bottom of the tub, place the pieces of Meat completely unsalted on their sides in [the tub] so far apart that they do not

[38]The appendix on butchering is a model of clarity. It will be of use to those museums that have food-preservation programs. Slaughtering time was generally in the month of November, when the moon was right. See advice in "About the Pigs": "one shall kill the Pig in the first quarter or during the waxing of the moon."

touch one another, a second layer on top, sprinkle with salt where they will stand on top of each other and so on, then one pours Brine on it until all the Meat is well covered; and if the pieces should float to the top hold them down with something heavy. But one needs to check every 6 to 8 days if the Brine is bloody, thick, or filmy and if so pour off all the Brine and boil it, skimming it well, and when it is cold pour it back in the tub; in this way the Meat will not become as salty or as hard as the other. Many place the best and fattiest pieces on the bottom because they can stand the salt better than the lean pieces, yes not only better (because the salt even takes away the rankness) but improve [by this method], whereas when you leave the lean pieces for the longest time in the Brine they will become hard and rough. However, everyone should do this according to his own desire.

About smoking the Meat.

The Meat that one wants to smoke should be rubbed with salt first but not as hard [with as much salt] as that which one places in the tub; when it is rubbed one places it in a Tub to pickle. Some leave it in this way for 14, 12, 10, or 8 days, but 3 days and 3 nights is enough for all. Some place the Meat in bags of loosely woven linen or canvas, others tie it in grey paper, some roll it in Bran or Sawdust, but it is best to hang it without one thing or another because then it smokes through much better. Leave it hanging until the Month of March then take advantage of a clear dry day, take it down, scrub off the soot with clean water and let it dry in the Sun or Wind for a whole day, then hang it in the kitchen on the Beams near the Chimney until you need it. But if you also smoke the fatty rib pieces, the ones that are called the *Pater* pieces [the best pieces], those and the Tongues, Hams, and Bacon may be taken from the smoke a month or 6 weeks earlier than the other [pieces].

About the Pigs.

One shall kill the Pig in the first quarter or during the waxing of the Moon. So that the Meat or Bacon will be drier and firmer one shall not give it anything to drink 24 hours or a day and night beforehand because of the drinking the Brine will attract more liquid. And if you also leave the Pig without food for a 24-hour period the Meat will be better and tastier to eat.

The less bones and knuckles you leave in the Meat the better it is because that makes the Brine keep [for a] longer [period of time] and the Meat stays tastier without spoiling, similarly to when [the pig] is killed while half thirsty and hungry.

When the Pig is killed some have it butchered immediately to salt it, after they have first soaked it in water to extract the blood, but it is better to hang it for 24 hours and to extract the blood because that way the Meat is healthier and drier. After that it is butchered according to everyone's desire, large or small, well salted and packed down to keep and a heavy weight is placed on top to keep [it] well.

In Some Countries the Pork is not cut into pieces but [the pig] is cut into two parts and salted on plates or in troughs 2 or 3 days, then it is hung on the ceiling. It is said that it is firmer and tastier.

From a Pig one can prepare many tasty and sweet dishes for the Winter and also to use the whole year around, such as either smoked or pickled Bacon from Hams, Shanks, with Herbs or in *Hutspot*.

One leaves the Hams and Shoulders in the Salt for 9 or 10 days and then one hangs them in the smoke with the Head or the Hams from the Jawbones [see last lines of the next section "From the meat on the Head."] The Back and the side-Bacon with the Rib pieces can be salted in a tub in order to prepare one's food and pottage on a winter's day and to cook with Carrots, Turnips, Cabbage, Pot-Herbs and other Herbs and also to cook with it little bags of Groats-flour.

When the Pig has been salted it sometimes happens that the Brine turns red and bloody after a while. Pour this off. Either one cooks this and skims it and lets it get cold and pours it on the Meat again or one throws it out and pours new Brine on [the meat] which one can make oneself from Salt and River or clear well-water until a fresh Hen egg floats in it or swims on it. Then it is salty enough.

From the Offal.

From the meat on the Head.

To press the Head-meat into the [shape of a] cheese you take the Head after it has been thoroughly boiled in water, cut off the Meat from the bones and remove the glands or in another way tie the Head up and let it cook until done (some take also the lung and liver of the Animal and the Heart. When the Head is done until the bones fall out, place it on a cutting board and sort out the glands [until all have been removed] and then chop [the meat] but not too fine, then spice with Salt, Pepper, Nutmeg, and Cloves, each to his liking, then tie securely in a cloth and return to the boiling kettle from which the fat has been skimmed, to be reheated completely and placed in a press with a lot of weight on top.

The Head-meat is eaten like this cold with Vinegar; also it is stewed sometimes with sour or sweet Apples. The Head of the Pig is chopped in half and salted but it cannot last long. It is sometimes boiled, the bones removed and pressed together, then it is spiced to make Pickled Pork [which is] placed in Beer-Vinegar. The Jawbones are sometimes hung in the smoke which are called *kinnebacks-hammetjes* [jawbone-hams].

To keep Head-meat.

Place it by itself in a large earthenware Stewing-pan and pour onto [it] very weak Wine-vinegar which is not very sour or good Beer-vinegar with some slices of Horseradish on it; it should always stay covered with Vinegar.

To roll Tripe.

Take the Tripe when it is thoroughly cleaned, cut it in pieces according to the size of the Rolls you want, add to it Salt, Pepper, Sage, and some Nutmeg and Cloves and ample Fat, cut into long pieces. Also one can add Lean Meat sliced thin or some Rice, and sew it tightly shut and cook [until] very well done and then press [it].

When one wants to use this Tripe cut it in slices which are fried in the pan with fried Apple slices.

Also this Tripe [is used] not rolled, only cut into pieces and cooked as described before and put away. When this is used, cut into long strips and stew with sour Apples and Currants.

The Pig's-stomach is filled with Groats and Fat and cooked like the Gut-Puddings or otherwise just the way it is.

From the Feet.

Steam off completely the hair from the Feet and when the hooves are chopped off they [the feet] are cooked until well done, so that the knuckles and bones fall out, then that [the meat] is chopped and pressed until the broth runs out clear and then put away like the Tripe. When one wants to eat these, just heat them in water with a sauce of Butter, Vinegar, and Sugar; one can fry these in the pan and [serve] the same sauce over it.

One also stews them in a pot with some Rhenish wine, Butter, Currants, and crushed Cloves.

One treats the Muzzle in the same way.

The Pigs-Feet are cooked and then placed in Vinegar [to make] Pickled Feet.

To preserve the Tripe, Feet, and Muzzle, and to keep it from getting moldy and spoiling.

Take four *mingelen* sweet Whey, pour it in an earthenware pot and let it boil, but one has to stay with it to skim as long as foam appears, then add proportionately whole Pepper, a few blades of Mace, some whole Cloves, a Nutmeg cut into 4 or 6 pieces. Let it boil together, take it off [the fire] and let it stand to settle until it is cold, pour it off entirely and add 3 pints of Wine-Vinegar. It is good.

Some also place it [the tripe, feet and muzzle] in Beer-Vinegar with slices of Horseradish.

To make Pig's Sausages.

Take three *pond* of chopped Meat, two Nutmegs, a *loot* Pepper not too finely crushed, a handful of Salt. Knead this together well, fill the intestines not too stiffly; if you want to hang these in the smoke you have to take thicker intestines and place [the sausage] for 2 or 3 days in the brine. One can also use half the amount in Mutton.

To make Beef-sausages.

In this same manner one makes also Beef-sausages; but one adds also some dried Sage (rubbed fine) but not in those which one wants to hang in the smoke, but those must be spiced with Pepper and stuffed into very thick intestines, covered with grey paper, and hung at the side of the Chimney.

To make Groats-gut puddings.

Take Barley Groats as many cups as you wish, add to it hot water that is boiling, let it stand to swell until the Groats are nicely swollen, then take Pig's-blood, heated until luke-warm and poured through a cloth until the Groats are completely red, for each cup [use] a Nutmeg, a quarter *loot* Cloves crushed fine and Salt as appropriate, stir well with Pig's lard or Kidney Suet, fill Clean Intestines very thin so that the Gut Pudding is only half full. They will not boil out [of the intestines in this way]; they have to boil gently for an hour. Some also take a portion of these prepared Groats and mash it with finely mashed Pig or Beef liver, but then it should be spiced and salted a little more and also [the intestines should be] stuffed more.

To make *Slabberaen* gut puddings.[39]

Take Oats groats, moisten the Groats with clean hot water, for each cup [use] a quarter *pond* Currants, a Nutmeg, and a half *loot* Cinnamon crushed, some Salt and mix in some Beef fat, smaller pieces than [for] the other Gut Puddings, and [make it] very soft, and thinly stuff the intestines. Let it boil for a good half hour, because they burst very easily.

To make Pig's Liver-gut puddings.

Take Pig-Liver, boil it until done, skim it. When it is cold grate it fine, take half *pint* sweet Milk, a *stuyver* stale White-bread, cut off the crust,

[39]Word play with *slobber,* as in slobbering at the mouth. These sausages burst quickly and are sloppy.

grate it fine, and place it in the Milk; let it boil together until it is a thick porridge, also put a good piece of Butter in the porridge; when it is almost cold stir in the Liver, then take 9 or 10 Eggs well beaten, a little Salt, Pepper, Nutmeg, Cloves and Mace finely crushed, and some melted Butter, all together well mixed, stuff the Intestines without forgetting the Pig's-lard and let them cook for an hour.

THE END OF THE DUTCH BUTCHERING TIME.

21. *Still Life with Confectionery and Pastries and Scene of the Rich Man and Lazarus,* Osias Beert the Elder. More than enough to satisfy a sweet tooth, the confections and pastries in this painting are made by a professional baker/confectioner. In the foreground are comfits: candied seeds and spices. Preserved sugared fruits as described in "The Sensible Confectioner" are part of the display. Courtesy Galerie Hoogsteder BV, 's-Gravenhage.

THE SENSIBLE CONFECTIONER.

Instructing how good and useful Preserves can be made from all sorts of Fruits, Roots, Flowers, and Leaves Etc.

To make Preserves.

The Sugar or the Honey with which one wants to preserve must be cleared or cleaned with the whites of Eggs and Rainwater, skim well and boil until it begins to lime [glue — becomes viscous like bird lime][40] or spin.

To candy green Walnuts.

Pick the Nuts on St. John['s Day: June 24] before the pit is hard, with a small pin prick several holes in them, soak them for 9 or 10 days and refresh [the water] often then boil in a little water and then boil in Sugar or Syrup, but at least four times as long as for Lemons or Orange, when the membrane is removed and Cloves or Cinnamon have been stuck in them, cook them adding some Honey or Sugar once in a while as they boil away, then leave in the Syrup. You can keep them for a long time this way.

[40]In the seventeenth century, when sugar was not as highly refined as it is now, it was necessary to clarify the sugar before preserving and candying. Technically, of course, one clarifies sugar syrup. Use 1 egg white to clarify 2 pounds of sugar if the need arises for clarification. (Hess, 225.) *Lijmen* in Dutch means "to glue," but it also refers to the practice of putting a sticky substance on a branch in order to catch birds. The implication is that the sugar syrup becomes viscous.

To pickle Gherkins or small Cucumbers which are delicious.

Take small Cucumbers when they are in season, take 2 or 3 handfuls of Salt, put those in the water in which you are going to soak the Cucumbers for half an hour to wash them, and then wash them clean without handling them very much, otherwise they lose their prime then [remove] from the water onto an earthenware colander, and when they are well drained put them in a Bottle or gray earthenware Pot, between each layer of Cucumber you put Mace, Pepper, Cloves, and slices of Horseradish, Fennel, and Laurel-leaves until your Bottle or Pot is full, add to it the best Wine-vinegar so that they are covered completely; one should not put these in the cellar, but they are better in a dry place.

To candy half Apples dry.

Take good and firm Apples, cut them in half, peel them, core them, but do not peel them in the round, but oblong. Then take cleared Sugar-Syrup, put the half Apples in it and let it boil together until the Syrup thickens. [When] the Apples seem to have become pulpy they have to be taken out of the Syrup with a spoon as dry as you can [without liquid] and placed on Tins in a warm *stoof* and when dry on top turned over with a knife and left until they are completely dry. You can sift finely pounded sugar over it to dry it better. Keep them in a dry place between clean paper.

To candy Pears wet.

Take Muscat-pears or others which have no stone inside and are also rather dry; peel them but the stem should stay on. Boil or cook them in clear water but not too soft or too well done, take them from the water and let them drain, pour over it sifted finely pounded sugar until they are covered; let them stand a day, pour off the Syrup when it becomes thin, cook it again until [it is a] thick Syrup, then pour over the Pears again. Do this as many times until the Syrup stays thick. Leave them in there. They are good.

To candy Pears dry.

Take Pears and treat them as described before, thin the Syrup again with water, let them boil together, take out the Pears while hot, place them on tins as described for the Apples. Note that when the Preserves have almost soaked up the Sugar it is then time [to remove them]; because otherwise they become fatty, and because of that they cannot dry, and the fattiness will not go away, and they also lose their clarity because of that.

To Candy Pears.

Take peeled Pears, sprinkle them with finely pounded Sugar, place them on a board in a tin platter, place them in the Oven, pour off the juices, turn them over, sprinkle with more sifted Sugar, sprinkle with Rosewater, repeat 3 or 4 times turning and sugaring until they are almost dry. Place them on a sieve which has been turned upside down in a warm Oven from which the Bread has been removed until they are dry, then you can save them for a whole year.

To candy Quinces.

Take as many Quinces as Sugar [equal amounts by weight], remove peels and cores, cook them in a covered pot on a low fire, add to it some Cinnamon cut fine, stir once in a while until they have color on all sides, when the Sugar has cooked to the thickness of jellied broth take them from the fire; the thicker the Syrup is the longer the Quinces will take and the longer they cook the brighter their color will be.

To candy half Quinces, in another manner.

Take Quinces (not too yellow or too ripe) freshly picked, cut them in half, remove the cores and peel them, clear three *pond* of finely pounded sugar with three *pints* of water, add to it 5 *pond* of halved Quinces, let them cook together until one or two drops of the Syrup (which have been left to cool on a dinner plate) can be lifted up like a jelly, place the halved Quinces in pots, pour on the Syrup; when cold tie them up and store them.

To make red Marmalade from Quinces.

Take Quinces, peel them and cut them in pieces, remove the cores and pits, boil them together with a little Wine until pulp, and for twelve *pond* of pulp take 8 *pond* of cleared Sugar, mix it well; let it boil, stir it steadily until it is thick enough, it should fall all at once from a tin platter, put it then in [splint][41] boxes. It is agreeable.

To make a red Marmalade in another manner.

Take ten *pond* Quinces cut in half, take out the seeds and peels, then take nine *pond* Sugar with a *mingelen* Rainwater, put this all together in a pan, let it cook on a slow fire, stir it up and cover it but so that water [steam] can escape; the longer they cook the redder they will be, and when they are done cut them across so that the Syrup can be absorbed and bring uniform color. Cool a little of the Syrup and when it thickens break up your Quinces as small as possible. Try some when it is dished up, if you can cut it with a knife without it [the quince] sticking then it is right to be put in [splint] boxes to save.

Still another kind of red Marmalade.

The Quinces peeled and cut into pieces and then grated and pressed, take that juice [from the pressing] with a half a pitcher of water and two *pond* Loaf-sugar, boil it together with that Sugar to make a Syrup and skim well, add the Quinces [another batch]; cover it well, let it boil until they are red, rub them fine, put them back to boil, dish up; the fewer at the same time the better.

To make white Marmalade, or Quince-meat.

Take unpeeled quinces, boil them in a basin with water until the skin bursts, then take them out, peel them and cut off the fruit meat until you

[41]Flat, low splint boxes, the kind we now call "Shaker boxes," are used for keeping dry preserves (see illustration 22).

22. *Still Life with Sweetmeats,* Juan van der hamel y Leon. Preserved fruits and confections are packed into splint boxes for storage. Courtesy Museum of Fine Arts, Boston, M. Theresa B. Hopkins Fund.

reach the core; then mash this [the cores] and rub through a sieve which is not too fine to keep the stoniness out, you will dry [the pulp] in a basin on the fire but stir steadily; when it is dried somewhat you take for each *pond* a *pond* of Sugar which has been cleared with water and [boiled] to a rather thick syrup; when you take it off the fire mix it [the syrup and the pulp] together and let it boil together for a little [while]. Spoon it in [splint] boxes while warm and place them in a warm *stoof* until it forms a crust. The [splint] boxes may also not be closed; store them for later use. Some take one and a quarter *pond* finely crushed Loaf-sugar and mix that with only a *pond* of the [fruit] meat, then it is rubbed through a sieve as mentioned above and boiled for a little while; this Marmalade will be whiter but has to stand in the *stoof* for a longer time.

To make Quince *koeckjes* [little cakes].

Take whole Quinces, rub them clean, cook them in water, let them boil unpeeled until they are soft, take them out, cover them with a cloth until they are luke-warm, remove the skins also the core and the hard parts and mash them [the quinces] very fine, take as much Sugar as [you have] Quince pulp, mix together and place on the fire, let it boil; when it has been boiled sprinkle a clean board with Sugar and place it on there, form little cakes. Let them cool, place them on a *stoof* with fire until they are dry; you can save them in clean paper as long as you please.

To make Quince-pieces with Lemons.

Take a *pond* of juice from Quinces, juice of two Lemons, and three *pond* of Loaf-Sugar, let it boil until it has foamed thoroughly then take five *pond* of clean peeled Quinces, cut as big as one wants, grate the yellow peel of two Lemons then cook together in clean water until it threads and [is] left in the Syrup. Is very good.

To preserve Apricots, Peaches, and Plums.

Take Apricots, Peaches, or Plums of each a *pond* cleared as before and cook it together until the thickness of a medium Syrup, let it cool and save in pots, is good.[42]

To preserve Black Cherries, Morella Cherries, and Cherries.

For 6 *pond* Morella or Cherries (of which half the stems have been cut off) take four *pond* cleared Sugar (as has been explained) with water and white of an Egg then cooked together gently in the Syrup, but [make sure] they do not burst, until the Sugar begins to thread then place warm in glazed pots with the stems up and the Syrup poured over.

[42]There obviously is a mistake in this recipe: the sugar was omitted. To make a proper preserve, use a pound each of fruit and sugar.

To preserve Cherries, Black cherries, and Morella cherries in another manner.

Take a *pond* of Black Cherry juice, three *pond* of Loaf-sugar, boiled together until it has foamed; then [add] six *pond* clean Cherries with the stems, let it boil gently until it limes [glues or becomes viscous] and remove. One should not let tin or copper come near any Preserves.

To make Morella juice.

Press the juice from the Morella, for 5 *pond* of Juice take one and a half *pond* Sugar and cook it together, skim it clean, then poured in Bottles and when cold closed, keeps for a long time. Mulberries are done in this manner also.

To make Cherry sauce.

Take Black Cherries, let them boil in Wine, rub them through a Hair Sieve, then boil again until it thickens stirring steadily; for 3 *pond* of such Sauce take two and a half *pond* of Sugar, boil it until it is of medium thickness. One also makes this with spices; when it is still warm one takes for one *pond* [sauce] a *loot* of Cloves and Cinnamon, a quarter *loot* Ginger and Galangal; an eighth of a *loot* Nutmeg, Mace, and Grains of Paradise: This Black Cherry sauce strengthens the heart.

To preserve the fruit-marrow of Cherries, Plums, Apricots, etc. for a whole year.

Take Cherries that are somewhat sour, take off the stems, boil them in an earthenware pot without liquid on a low fire, when they start to cook in their own juice stir them so that they do not burn, they are done when the outer skin comes off and the meat has become a thick porridge; let them cool and rub them through a turned-over Sieve, take the resulting porridge and spread it on glazed tiles, let it dry this way in the sun or in an oven when the bread has been removed, take it from the dish [presumably the dish in which it is dried in an oven] and save it; it is good to create an appetite, and to cool off in hot Fevers.

To preserve whole Currants.

Take Currants, remove them from the stems, place them in a pitcher, let it [the pitcher with contents] boil in a kettle with water, tightly close the pitcher; when the Berries are done then drain them through a Sieve; for a *pond* and a half of juice take two *pond* of Sugar and a small bowl of Rain-water, let that boil, add the whole Berries, let it boil gently until it begins to lime [glue — or become viscous] and then until it limes [gets very viscous] well.

To make a Syrup of Currants, or *Rob de Rubes.*[43]

Remove the Currants from the stems, squeeze it through a thick gauze cloth so that you have nothing but pure juice in which there are no stones or impurities, for each *pint* of juice take three quarter *pond* of Sugar, let it boil together on a small fire stirring steadily with a spatula until it starts to stick to the top of the spatula and then put into pots. Is good for hot Fevers, and there has not been found a better cooling than this for the Tongue.

To make a Syrup of Currants.

Take three *pond* of Currant juice and two *pond* of Sugar, boil it together to a thin Syrup: this Syrup is good for all hot Fevers, in the pestilence: it quenches thirst, it strengthens the Heart, the Stomach and the Liver in all hot illnesses.

To make red Currant juice.

Take red Currants, remove them from the stems and rub them fine in a bowl then squeeze them through a cloth, take that juice and put it in a bottle, set it in the sunshine to distill, but the Bottle must be full, and place a medlar, in which a cross has been cut, on the mouth of the Bottle

---

[43]According to *Larousse Gastronomique*, rob is "fruit juice thickened by evaporation to the consistency of honey." *Rubes* is probably *ribes*, the Latin name for currant.

and the Bottle will boil over regularly and when some [juice] has boiled out add more juice often until all of it is clear, then add some Sugar-Candy syrup and save it to stew Apples, Pears, Quinces or something else; it also gives a pleasant taste to add to Wine or to stew Carps.

To pickle Quinces so that they do not spoil.

Take the cores and peels of Quinces, boil them in stream or well-water until it is a medium mush, add to it some Cloves, Cinnamon, and Mace and when you have rubbed the wooliness off the Quinces pack them in a pot or small barrel, pour on that juice with peels and all until they are covered, then close [the pot or barrel] tightly. When you want to use them you must take them out with a wooden spoon. One can also cook the Quinces in the juice for a while before they are put up but then they turn brownish.

THE END

23. Baked Goods. Composite photo of baked goods, pastries, and sweets not portrayed in the other illustrations. Starting at eleven o'-clock: *krul* and crullers, *speculaas* with shaved almonds, rusks, *taai-taai*, wooden mold for *speculaas* with unmolded cookie, little quince cakes, syrup wafers, and four kinds of *olie-koecken*. In the middle a modern cast-iron *poffertjes* pan with *poffertjes*. Photo by Wally McFall.

RECIPES FOR MODERN KITCHENS

I OFFER TWO DOZEN RECIPES which either have been adapted from *The Sensible Cook* or are in some significant way connected with the Dutch colonial past. Although in general the recipes in the cookbook are very clear, some might feel more comfortable with a modern version. I have given an explanation, where appropriate, regarding the history of those recipes that are not from the book. The serving suggestions for modern meals are mine.

I chose the entries for both sections so that at least some comparisons can be made between the original recipe from *The Sensible Cook* and a New Netherland counterpart; for example, Meatballs in Head Lettuce and Forced Meatballs. In some other cases, my selection was made because the recipe is still used in either or both countries; for example, coleslaw, Shoemaker's *taert*, or hash. I included four versions of *olie-koecken* because these fritters feature prominently in New Netherlandish celebrations. Each recipe is distinctly different. All the recipes in the second section help us in creating a clearer picture of the foodways of New Netherland.

Recipes from The Sensible Cook.

Beef *Hutspot* with Ginger.

6 tablespoons butter
2 pounds stew beef
2 tablespoons fresh ginger, peeled and finely chopped
¼ teaspoon ground mace

1 teaspoon salt, or more, to taste
½ cup chopped parsley

Melt the butter and brown the meat cubes on all sides. Add the ginger and mace just before you are finished browning the meat. When the meat is brown, add enough water to almost cover. Bring to a boil and then reduce the heat. Simmer for 45 minutes to an hour or until the meat is tender. Check every once in a while to see if water needs to be added. Add the parsley and salt and stir to combine. Serve with rice and spinach, seasoned with nutmeg; or with potatoes and parsleyed carrots. Serves 4 to 6.

Chicken with Green Vegetables.

3 pounds chicken, cut into small serving pieces
1 pound boneless lamb stew meat, cut into ½ inch cubes
Salt to taste
About ½ pound of a prepared meatloaf mixture, or your favorite commercial breakfast sausage patties, shaped into small flat meatballs of about 2 inches in diameter
1 cut Romaine lettuce, finely cut
1 cup sorrel, if available, finely cut
1 cup celery with leaves, thinly sliced
½ pound asparagus, cleaned; thawed, frozen asparagus may be substituted

In a large pan combine the chicken pieces and the lamb stew meat. Cover with water, add salt, and bring to a boil. Carefully skim off the foam. Reduce the heat and gently simmer for about 40 minutes. In the meantime, nicely brown the meatballs on both sides in a frying pan and add them to the chicken and lamb. When the chicken is done, pour off about half of the broth (or less if you like a more soupy consistency) and save for another use. Add the cut vegetables to the meat mixture. Cook for about five minutes more and serve straight from the pot. A hot loaf of crusty bread is the perfect accompaniment. Serves 4 to 6.

Chicken with Orange.

3 pounds chicken, whole and skinned
1½ teaspoons salt
1 lemon, cut in half
Orange marmalade
1 to 2 teaspoons cinnamon

Rub the chicken all over with the cut lemon halves. Salt the chicken. With a pastry brush, coat it with the marmalade, as if you were coating it with barbecue sauce. Place it in a roasting pan and roast in the oven at 375 degrees for about 40 minutes. Coat the chicken with more marmalade as it cooks. Watch out for burning; cover very brown parts with foil. Remove the bird and dust it with the cinnamon and return to the oven for 5 minutes. This is an unusual taste, but not as outlandish as you might think. Serve with baked sweet potatoes and buttered, steamed green beans, seasoned lightly with freshly grated nutmeg. Serves 4.

Hash.

This is a recipe for leftover cooked meats. Nowadays beef or pork is used, but *The Sensible Cook* suggests using veal, chicken, or turkey as well. This is a modern version. *Hachee* is still a popular dish in the Netherlands and so is hash in the United States.

3 tablespoons butter or margarine
3 medium onions, chopped
About 2 cups leftover gravy from which the fat has been removed,
    thinned with water or broth, if necessary, to make 2 cups
2 tablespoons red wine vinegar, or more to taste
2 bay leaves
2 cups or so leftover meat, either beef or pork, cut into small pieces
Salt and freshly ground pepper

Brown the butter and fry the onions until nicely browned. Add the gravy, vinegar, bay leaves, and the leftover meat. Bring to a boil and reduce heat. Simmer gently for about ½ hour. Taste and adjust seasonings with salt and pepper. If desired, the sauce may be thickened with corn-starch or flour. Serve with mashed potatoes, red cabbage or beets, and apple sauce. Serves 4.

Kandeel.

1 bottle dry Rhine or Moselle wine
5 whole cloves
¼ teaspoon mace
Pinch of grated nutmeg
1 3-inch cinnamon stick
2 tablespoons sugar or more to taste
6 egg yolks

Gently simmer the spices and sugar in the wine for about 30 minutes. In the meantime, beat the egg yolks until they are thick and light-colored. Strain the wine, discard the spices, and add some of the hot wine to the egg yolks. Add that mixture back to the spiced wine and combine. Return to very low heat and stir until the mixture is thickened. Remove immediately. Serve in porcelain cups; if you have them, use cups without handles. It can also be served cold, which might be more palatable to modern tastes, because of the drink's odd contrast of the custardy texture and the wine flavor.

Meatballs in Head Lettuce.

1 pound ground veal
2 slices of bread soaked in milk and squeezed dry
1 egg, whole
⅛ teaspoon freshly grated nutmeg
Salt and freshly ground pepper to taste
4 small heads of Boston lettuce
4 egg yolks
Thread for tying
6 tablespoons of butter or margarine

Combine ground veal, soaked bread, and egg. Season with nutmeg, salt, and pepper. Shape into 4 meatballs. Thoroughly wash the heads of lettuce. Open them up and remove a few leaves to create a hollow in the middle where the meatball will fit. Place the meatball inside. With your finger poke a hole into it and place the egg yolk in the middle of the meatball. Gently and carefully close and smooth the lettuce leaves around it to form a ball. Tie with string to keep in place. Melt the butter and gently brown the lettuce balls on all sides. Add ½ cup water and cover the pan. Braise the meatballs over low heat until done, about 40 minutes or so. When done the egg yolk will have cooked and is a pretty surprise in the middle. Serve with a mixture of parsleyed carrots and parsnips — cut into 3-inch sticks — which have been cooked together, and boiled potatoes.

Olie-koecken.

The batter for *olie-koecken* should be thick and heavy to stir. Do not make them too small; they should be at least 2 inches in diameter. When feeding a crowd it is better to cut them in half or quarters, than to make them in a smaller size, because it is difficult to distribute the ingredients evenly.

> *3 packages dry yeast*
> *½ cup warm (105 – 115 degrees) water and a pinch of sugar for the yeast*
> *8 tablespoons butter*
> *1¾ cups raisins*
> *4 cups flour*
> *¼ teaspoon salt*
> *1 tablespoon cinnamon*
> *½ teaspoon cloves*
> *½ teaspoon ground ginger*
> *1½ cups milk*
> *1 cup whole almonds without brown skins*
> *3 medium Granny Smith apples, peeled and cut into small slivers*
> *Oil for deep-frying*

Sprinkle the yeast on the water in a small bowl and sprinkle with the sugar. Let it stand for a moment, then stir to dissolve the yeast. Set aside in a warm place. In the meantime, melt the butter and cool. Place the raisins in a saucepan, cover with water, and bring to a boil. Allow them to boil for a minute and turn off the heat. Let them stand for five minutes and drain. Pat them dry with paper towels and mix them with a tablespoon of flour. Place the rest of the flour in a large bowl, stir in the salt, cinnamon, cloves, and ginger, make a well in the middle and pour in the yeast. Stir from the middle and slowly add the melted butter and the milk. The dough should be very thick and hard to stir. Then add raisins, apples, and almonds and combine thoroughly. Allow this batter to rise for about an hour. When doubled in bulk, stir down the dough. Heat the oil to 350 degrees. Scoop out a heaping tablespoon of dough and push it off the spoon with the aid of another spoon and let it (carefully) drop into the hot oil. They should be at least 2 inches in diameter. Fry the *olie-koecken* for about 5 minutes on each side. Drain on paper towels. The original recipe does not tell us to sprinkle or roll them in sugar. They are very good plain, but if you prefer you can dust them with confectioners' sugar. Makes about 30.

Pear *taert.*

½ cup currants
2 cups flour
⅓ cup light brown sugar, firmly packed
11 tablespoons cold butter (do not use margarine)
2 egg yolks, lightly beaten with a fork
10 – 12 small pears, peeled, cut in quarters and then into 2 or 3
*   lengthwise slices*
⅓ – ½ cup white sugar, depending on the sweetness of the pears
½ teaspoon ground ginger
1 teaspoon cinnamon

Place the currants in a small saucepan. Cover with water and bring to a boil. Allow them to boil for a minute and turn off the heat. Let them soak for about 5 minutes. Drain thoroughly and set aside. Preheat the oven to 375 degrees. Combine flour, salt, and sugar, and cut in butter with a dough blender or two knives until it resembles coarse meal. Stir in egg yolks. Knead this mixture until smooth. This takes quite a bit of kneading (you might want to use two hands). Press the dough out on the bottom and sides of an 8- or 9-inch springform pan. Neatly finish the rim. In a large bowl gently combine the pear slices with the spices, sugar, and currants. Carefully arrange the fruits in the crust. Bake for about 30–40 minutes, or until the crust is golden. Cool and serve.

Pancakes, the Best.

6 eggs
Water
¼ teaspoon each ground cloves, cinnamon, mace, and nutmeg
Pinch of salt
4 cups flour
Butter for frying

Beat the eggs with a little water until light. Measure; you should have at least 2 cups of liquid. If not, add some more water. Combine spices and salt and flour, stir in the liquid to make a smooth batter which, if you prefer thinner pancakes, can be diluted with water. Fry in butter in a frying pan. Make them any size you like.

Pancakes with Currants.

4 cups flour
2 cups milk or more
1 cup currants
1 tablespoon cinnamon
Butter for frying

Make a batter from the above ingredients. If you prefer thinner pancakes, the batter can be diluted with more milk. Fry the pancakes in butter in a frying pan. Make them any size you like.

Little Quince Cakes.

4 quinces, well scrubbed
Water and sugar

Place the quinces in a saucepan and cover with water. Bring to a boil
and gently boil for about 25 minutes or until tender and the skins start
to burst. Remove and cover with paper towels. Cool until lukewarm.
Cut into quarters, remove core and any hard parts. Scrape the pulp into
a bowl, discard skins, and mash thoroughly. Weigh the pulp and mix
with an equal amount of sugar. Place in a heavy saucepan and bring to
a full boil. Boil, while stirring constantly until the mixture thickens and
withdraws from the sides of the pan (about 5 minutes). Sprinkle a baking sheet thickly with sugar. Spread the hot quince mixture upon the
sugar in an even layer about ⅙ inch thick, and cool. When the mixture
is cool enough to touch, cut it into neat 1-inch squares. Sprinkle another
baking sheet with sugar and place the squares upside down onto the
sugar. Heat the oven to "warm" about 220 to 250 degrees. Sprinkle the
squares lightly with sugar and place in the warm oven to dry. Turn the
oven off, but turn the light on. The drying will take several hours. Every
hour or so, turn over the squares and sprinkle them lightly with sugar
if they still seem very moist. It is best to leave them in the oven overnight
with the oven light on. In the morning when they are no longer sticky,
place them between tissue paper in an airtight container and store in a
cool place. They will keep for months. Makes at least 24 1-inch
squares.

Shoemaker's *Taert*

This recipe still appears in modern Dutch cookbooks in much the same
form as we find it in *The Sensible Cook*.

10 sweet/sour apples, peeled, cored, and cut into chunks
1 cup raisins
5 tablespoons butter, melted, plus additional butter for greasing the pan
Sugar to taste
4 egg yolks
4 egg whites, stiffly beaten
1 – 1½ cups plain dry breadcrumbs

Boil or steam the apples without water until very tender. This requires supervision, otherwise they will burn. Mash the apples and taste them. Add as much sugar as you think is necessary. Add the raisins and butter, then the yolks, and finally gently fold in the egg whites and incorporate thoroughly. Butter a 9-inch springform pan very carefully and sprinkle with bread crumbs to make an even coating. Pour half the apple mixture in the prepared pan and sprinkle the top with more bread crumbs. Then add the remainder of the apple mixture and top with an even layer of bread crumbs. Bake at 350 degrees for about 45 to 60 minutes until the cake is firm and light brown. Remove, cool, and remove ring. Serve cut into wedges with or without a dollop of sweetened whipped cream.

Recipes from the Dutch Colonial Past.

Butter Chicken.

The recipe comes from Anna de Peyster's manuscript. It reads in part: "Take two chickens pickt them Very Clean & boyle them with a blade of mace & a Little Salt then take them of[f] [the Spit] & Cut them in pieces & put them into a toss up pan with a Little parslay Sherred a Little lemon peel . . . into your Dish Sauces . . . Some juice of Lemon . . . Garnish yr dish with Slices Lemon then Serve it up hot." I have adapted the recipe as follows:

> *3 pounds chicken, cut into pieces*
> *Blade of mace, or a pinch of ground mace*
> *1 teaspoon salt*
> *Water*
> *4 tablespoons butter*
> *2 tablespoons parsley*
> *1 tablespoon lemon juice*
> *Grated peel of 1 lemon*
> *1 cup of the broth in which the chicken was cooked*
> *Freshly ground pepper*
> *½ cup heavy cream*
> *1 lemon, cut into very thin slices for garnish*

Gently poach the chicken in enough water barely to cover the pieces, together with the mace and salt. When done, cool to touch; remove the
meat from the bones and cut into bite-size pieces. Melt the butter, add
the chicken pieces, stir and fry for a few minutes. Add parsley, lemon
juice, grated peel, and broth. Add some freshly ground, preferably
white, pepper. Gently simmer for 10 minutes. Add cream and reheat the
sauce but do not boil. If desired the sauce could be further thickened
with cornstarch or flour, but it is very good this way. Garnish your dish
with the lemon slices. Serve with boiled potatoes, a mixture of peas and
snow peas, and a salad.

Cabbage Salad.

I used the description in Peter Kalm's diary to create the following recipe (Kalm, 609).

> 2 cups green cabbage, cut into thin strips
> 2 cups red cabbage, cut into thin strips
> 1/3 cup wine vinegar
> 1/4 cup vegetable oil or 1/4 cup melted butter
> Salt and freshly ground pepper

Mix the above ingredients well ahead of dinner time so that the flavors
can marry.

Crullers, or Crulla.

Crullers always have been associated with Dutch cookery in America.
Anne Stevenson's recipe for them, entitled "Crulla" simply reads: "3
lbs. flour, 12 Eggs, 1 lb. sugar, a little butter & some Nutmeg." It makes
plain, rather crisp, fritters that can be dusted with confectioners' or cinnamon-sugar for extra flavor.

> 5 tablespoons butter   2 eggs
> 1/4 cup sugar   1/8 teaspoon freshly grated nutmeg
> 2 cups flour   Oil for deep-frying

24. *Sweet Meal*, Monogrammist BDC. In this still life with pancakes and waffles we recognize the sweet dishes for which recipes
have survived in America from the New Netherland period until
now. Courtesy Koninklijke Musea voor Schone Kunsten van Bel-
gie, Brussels. Copyright A. C. L. Brussel.

Cream butter and sugar, add eggs one at a time. Then add flour and nutmeg to make a smooth dough. Turn it out on a board and cut into 20
even pieces. Roll each piece out to a 6-inch rope. Fold the rope in half
and twist the ends around each other, leaving an opening in the middle.
An alternate method for shaping the crullers is to roll out the dough ¼-
inch thick. With a pie jagger cut into strips ½-inch wide and 3 inches
long. Twist two strips together. Heat the oil to 350 degrees and deep-fry
the crullers until golden and done. Remove and immediately sprinkle
with confectioners' or cinnamon-sugar, if desired. Makes 20.

Forced Meat Balls.

In Anne Stevenson's manuscript cookbook, I found this version of veal meatballs, which is spicier than the recipe in *The Sensible Cook*. For 2 pounds of veal, she includes the following: "½ Teaspoonful cayene Pepper ... black pepper, 2 Teaspoonsful of Salt ½ teaspoonful of Thyme ½ tablespoonful Onions and Celery or parsley — Of Orange Peal, Cloves — and alspice each a Teaspoonful & one Egg." I think that is a little too spicy for most palates, and I adapted the recipe as follows:

> *1 pound ground veal*
> *2 thin slices of bread soaked in water, squeezed dry*
> *1 egg*
> *1 tablespoon each minced onion and celery*
> *Pinch each of dried thyme, ground cloves, and ground allspice*
> *Grated peel of 1 orange*
> *1 teaspoon salt*
> *Freshly ground pepper*
> *Dash of cayenne pepper, if desired*

Combine all ingredients thoroughly and shape into balls. Fry in butter until nicely browned all around. Add some water and cover the pan. Simmer for about 20 minutes. Cut into one of the meatballs to check if they are done. Serves 4. Serve with parsleyed potatoes, sauteed zucchini, and yellow squash slices with a touch of garlic, and a salad of thinly sliced orange and red onion on a bed of Romaine lettuce.

Krullen.

Here is a completely different version of the cruller. The recipe is adapted from a nineteenth century Dutch cookbook that survived only as a fragment without a title page. This version resembles more closely Washington Irving's description in his "Legend of Sleepy Hollow." The author describes a Dutch tea table set for guests which included "Such heaped up platters of cakes of various and almost indescribable kinds, known only to experienced Dutch housewives. There was the doughty dough nut, the tenderer oly koek, and the crisp and crumbling cruller. . . . " (Irving, 287.) This recipe creates a crisp and crumbling cruller, or cork-screw *krul* (curl).

9 tablespoons butter (no substitutes)
1 egg
1²/₃ cups flour (tapped down)
2 tablespoons heavy cream, if needed

Cream the butter until light and fluffy. Add the egg and incorporate. Add the flour a little at a time. If the dough is too stiff, add some cream. Roll to a thickness of ⅙-inch and cut into strips of approximately ¾-inch wide (it does not matter how long they are). Twist around the handle of a wooden spoon to make a corkscrew curl. Gently slide off the handle into hot oil at about 350 degrees. Fry until golden brown and slightly puffed. Drain on paper towels. Sift confectioners' sugar over each curl before serving.

Lansing Recipe for *Oly-koecks.*

Among the papers of Mrs. Charles S. Hamlin (formerly Huibertje Lansing Pruyn) there was yet another version of *olie-koecken*, with also another, more anglicized version of the name. "One pound of sugar. half a pound of butter. One quart of milk. Six eggs. One & a half yeast cakes. As much fruit as you like. As much flour as will make a soft roll but no more for the less flour the better." She also suggests that the "citron & raisins ... [are] soaked in brandy over night."

1³/₄ cups raisins
1 cup citron
½ cup brandy
3 packages of dry yeast
¼ cup warm water (105 – 115 degrees)
Pinch of sugar
8 tablespoons butter
2 cups milk
1 cup sugar
3 egg yolks
3 egg whites, stiffly beaten
6 – 8 cups flour
½ teaspoon freshly grated nutmeg
Oil for deep-frying

The day before making the *oly-koeks*, combine the raisins and citron with the brandy and let the mixture soak overnight. Sprinkle the yeast on the warm water in a small bowl and sprinkle with the pinch of sugar. Let it stand for a moment then stir to dissolve the yeast. Set aside in a warm place. Before using, stir to dissolve the yeast. Warm milk and butter. Stir to dissolve butter and cool. Beat together the egg yolks and the sugar. Combine 2 cups flour with sugar and egg yolks; add egg whites, butter and milk mixture, and yeast; stir in more flour, a cup at a time, to make a soft dough. Let it rise in a warm, moist place until double in bulk. Add more flour if the dough is very sticky. Drain the fruits. Pat dry with paper towels. With well-floured hands, pinch off a portion of dough the size of an egg. Poke a hole in the dough ball and insert some fruit in the middle. Close. Deep fry the egg-sized dough balls in hot oil at 350 degrees until golden on all sides. Roll in confectioners' sugar before serving. They can be served hot or cold.

Olicooks (Albany method).

The spelling for the word *olie-koecken* in the New Netherlandish recipes differs from cook to cook. This recipe is adapted from Anne Stevenson's manuscript. I think she received it from the Van Rensselaer family because the exact same recipe appears in the Van Rensselaer cookbook. In that recipe it is suggested to use "as much milk as you like," whereas Anne Stevenson is more precise and says: "as muc[h] milk as you pleas[e], say near or quite 3 pints." Both recipes would make more than a hundred *olicooks*. Here is a more modest version. Please note that the batter for *olicooks* should be thick and heavy to stir.

> *3 packages of yeast*
> *¼ cup of warm water (105 – 115 degrees)*
> *Pinch of sugar*
> *½ cup butter*
> *¾ cup sugar*
> *3 eggs*
> *1 cup milk*
> *4 cups flour*
> *Additional sugar to coat the finished product*
> *Oil for deep-frying*

Sprinkle the yeast on the water in a small bowl and sprinkle with the pinch of sugar. Let it stand for a moment and stir to dissolve the yeast. Set aside in a warm place. Before using stir to dissolve yeast. Cream together the butter and sugar. Add the eggs one at a time. Add milk and yeast. Slowly stir in flour and combine thoroughly. Let the dough rise until truly double in bulk. Heat oil to about 350 degrees. Scoop out a heaping tablespoon of dough and push it off the spoon with the aid of another spoon and let it (carefully) drop into the hot oil. Cook slowly on one side until a deep brown, then turn and cook the other side. Remove and arrange on a thick layer of paper towels. Roll in sugar to coat. Cool and serve.

Oliebollen.

Oliebollen is the modern name for *olie-koecken*. I offer here my mother's recipe as a comparison. It is interesting to note that it is close to that in *The Sensible Cook. Oliebollen* are still served in the Netherlands today as part of the New Year's celebration. As noted for the recipe for *olie-koecken,* the batter for *oliebollen* should be thick and heavy to stir. *Oliebollen* should be at least 2 inches in diameter. They may be cut in half or quarters when serving a large number of people. Like doughnuts, they make excellent fair or bake-sale items.

> *3 packages of yeast*
> *¼ cup warm water (105 – 115 degrees)*
> *Pinch of sugar*
> *½ cup raisins*
> *½ cup currants*
> *3 – 4 cups flour*
> *1½ cups milk*
> *¼ teaspoon salt*
> *1 cup citron*
> *3 medium Granny Smith apples, peeled, cored, and cut into*
>   *small pieces*
> *Oil for deep-frying*

Sprinkle the yeast on the warm water in a small bowl and sprinkle it with the pinch of sugar. Let it stand for a moment and stir to dissolve the yeast. Set aside in a warm place. Bring the raisins and currants to a boil with a little water, take off the heat. Soak for 5 minutes. Drain. Pat dry with paper towels. Combine with a tablespoon of flour. Make a dough from the flour, milk, salt, and the yeast mixture, and add all the fruits. Let the dough rise for an hour in a warm place. Scoop out a heaping tablespoon of dough and push it off the spoon with the aid of another spoon and let it (carefully) drop into the hot (350 degrees) oil. Make the *oliebollen* at least 2 inches in diameter. Fry the *oliebollen* for about 5 minutes on each side, or until golden brown. Remove onto paper towels. Before serving, coat heavily with confectioners' sugar. Makes about 30. May be frozen or stored in an airtight container for a few days.

Pumpkin Cornmeal Pancakes.

This recipe was re-created from Peter Kalm's travel accounts of the year 1749. He tells us that a thick pancake "was made by taking the mashed pumpkin and mixing it with corn-meal after which it was ... fried." He found it "pleasing to my taste" (Kalm, 607).

> *1 cup all-purpose flour*
> *1 cup yellow cornmeal*
> *1 cup confectioners' sugar, plus extra sugar for topping*
> *½ teaspoon dried ground ginger*
> *½ teaspoon cinnamon*
> *1 cup mashed pumpkin, or use canned pumpkin*
> *2 eggs, lightly beaten with a fork*
> *2½–3 cups milk or more for thinner pancakes*
> *Butter for frying*

Combine dry ingredients in a large mixing bowl. Combine eggs and pumpkin. Beat into dry ingredients. Add milk slowly to make a smooth pancake batter. Heat some butter in a frying pan and pour some of the batter in. Swirl the batter around to make an evenly thick pancake. Cook on both sides until nicely browned. Serve hot, heavily dusted with confectioner's sugar.

Sappaen.

This simple mush is an integral part of the Dutch colonial past.

> *2 quarts water*
> *1 teaspoon salt*
> *1 cup yellow corn meal*

Bring the water and salt to a boil in a heavy pan over high heat. Stirring constantly, pour in the corn meal in a slow, thin stream so that the water continues to boil. Reduce the heat to low and, stirring frequently, simmer for 8 to 10 minutes. Serve with hot or cold milk poured over it. See illustration 11 for how to serve it in a communal bowl. Sugar or maple syrup may be added for flavor.

Small Seed Cakes.

A recipe adapted from the Anna de Peyster manuscript. She suggests to "Drop them in Lumps As big as Nutmegs."

> *½ cup butter*
> *1 cup sugar*
> *2 eggs*
> *2 cups flour*
> *1 tablespoon caraway seed, bruised in the mortar with a pestle*

Cream the butter with the sugar. Add eggs one by one and incorporate thoroughly. Add seeds and flour a little at a time, stir well. Use two teaspoons to shape the cookies about the size of a nutmeg and place them on a buttered baking sheet. Bake at 350 degrees for about 15 minutes, until the rims are browned. Makes 4 dozen.

Zoete Koek (Spiced Sweet Bread).

I found a recipe in Anne Stevenson's cookbook for "Honey Cooke." My version, which resembles hers but is made with brown sugar, is very similar in taste to the *zoete koeken,* for which the town of Deventer in the Netherlands is famous. In Steen's painting *The St. Nicholas Cele-bration* (illustration 12), the basket in the lower left-hand corner con-tains a long loaf-shaped *Deventer koek*.

1 cup dark brown sugar, packed
2 cups flour
1 teaspoon baking powder
1 teaspoon cinnamon
½ teaspoon freshly grated nutmeg
½ teaspoon ground cloves
1 cup milk

Sift the dry ingredients together into a large bowl. Slowly add the milk and stir to make a dough without lumps. Pour the dough into a greased 8 × 5 × 2¾-inch loaf pan and bake in a 350 degree oven for about one hour, or until a knife inserted comes out clean and the loaf is a deep brown. Cool and store. This is a dense loaf that keeps very well and im-proves in flavor and texture when stored in an airtight container for a few days.

GLOSSARY
BIBLIOGRAPHY
INDEX

Glossary

Note: For some of the herbs and spices an annotation about their use is added in parentheses from P. Nijland's *"Sensible Gardener,"* published simultaneously with the translated edition of *The Sensible Cook* in 1683.

Betony: *Stachys Betonica* (good for bladder and kidney ailments).

Bollabouche, sometimes ***billabusse,* or *bollebuysjes*:** tiny puffed pancakes fried in a special pan with indentations.

Borage: family of *Boraginaceae* (use flowers for salad or preserve in syrup).

Bugloss: *Anchusa officinalis* (use like borage).

Burnet: *Poterium Sanquisorba* (use for salad, but you can also put it in wine for a good taste and it gladdens the heart).

Calendula: family of *Compositae;* pot marigold, not to be confused with the regular marigold.

Catnip: a plant in the mint family (use in salad, because it has a lovely color).

Clary: *Salvia sclarea* (has leaves like sage with a strong smell).

Comfits: sugared seeds or spices. They are first dipped in a sugar syrup and then rolled into finely pounded sugar.

Deventer koek: a sturdy oblong cake made from rye flour, honey and at one time potash, now a chemical leavener, for which the town of Deventer is famous.

Duivekater: a large flat bread baked with or without raisins or currants, shaped like a shinbone or diamond.

Galangal, also galingale: the pungent, aromatic root stem of various East Indian plants of the ginger family.

Grains of paradise: sweet scented seeds from the African plant *Amomum meleguetta.*

Hutspot: hodgepodge or hotchpotch; a one-pot meal of a mixture of chopped ingredients.

125

Kandeel: a spiced drink like eggnog but made with wine.

Koe(c)k(en): a collective noun, indicating a baked good of diverse shape, prepared in a pot or pan, or baked in an oven from flour, water or milk, sweeteners, sometimes eggs, and seasonings. Depending on the method of preparation and ingredients, *koe(c)k* can be translated as cake, biscuit, hard gingerbread, fritter, or pancake. See Steen's *St. Nicholas Celebration* (illustration 12). The basket in the lower left corner is filled with *koe(c)k* in various shapes and sizes.

Koe(cx)kje(n): cookie. This includes anything that is made in the shape of a cookie, even though it would not normally be called "cookie" in English such as rice *koecxkens* (rice fritters), or quince *koeckjes* (little quince cakes).

Krap: a piece of pork with the bone in.

Lamb's lettuce: *Fedia* or *Valerianella olitoria;* corn salad, a European plant whose leaves are used in salad.

Last: 4,772.88 pounds.

Loot: about 14 grams.

Lovage: *Levisticum officinale;* known as Italian lovage or garden lovage, a European herb.

Medlar: *Mespilus germanica;* a small tree with brown fruit that is only edible after it begins to decay.

Mengel(e)(n), **sometimes** *mingel(en):* 1 liter.

Midriff: diaphragm.

Mud: one twenty-fifth part of an Amsterdam *last,* which when measuring rye equaled 4,400 pounds: 176 pounds.

Mutsje(n): 1½ deciliter.

Oblie: wafer, in New Netherland usage sometimes called hard waffle.

Oliebollen: present-day Dutch word for *olie-koecken.*

Olie-koecken, in New Netherland usage variously spelled as *olicook,* **or** *olykoecks:* one of the forerunners of the doughnut. A ball of dough prepared from flour, milk, and yeast, with or without sweetener and various fillings and deep fried in hot oil (for which they get their name), or lard.

Olipodrigo: from the Spanish *olla podrida;* a one-pot meal of many meats and vegetables.

Pastey(en): a sturdy raised crust containing a savory or sweet filling, with a lid. See illustration 13, in which you will not see the lids because the pastry shells have not yet been filled.

Pint: the same word in Dutch as in English, about ½ liter.

Poffertjes: present-day Dutch word for *bollabouche, billabusse,* or *bollebuysjes.*

Pond: the English pound, about 454 grams.

Puffert: raised pancake fried in a frying pan.

Purslane: *Portulaca oleracea.* A plant with fleshy, succulent leaves.

Rocket: *Eruca sativa;* a European plant, grown like spinach.

Roemer: a large footed wine glass.

Sandalwood: *Santalum album;* a low tree growing chiefly on the coast of Malabar and in the Indian archipelago. Looks like the privet. When the tree becomes old, the harder central wood acquires a yellow color and great fragrance, which is used for seasoning.

Sa(u)ppaen, **sometimes** *sapahn,* **or** *suppawn:* Indian cornmeal mush of pounded cornmeal and water, to which the Dutch added milk or buttermilk.

Speculaas: a hard, spiced small or large cookie, somewhat similar in taste to gingerbread. It is molded in carved wooden boards and unmolded before baking.

Stoof: a, enclosed chamber for drying foods; *b,* footwarmer, containing a pipkin with fire, which in addition to its intended purpose is also used to keep foods warm; *c,* chafing dish (see illustrations 5 and 17).

Stuyver: stiver; now one-twentieth part of a guilder.

Taai-taai: a chewy (*taai* means tough) Dutch version of the German *Lebkuchen.* It is molded in carved wooden boards and unmolded before baking.

Taert(en): a collective noun, indicating a baked good made from a short-crust dough containing a variety of mostly sweet, but sometimes savory fillings, resembling a tart, flan, patty, pie, or pastry. A *taert* usually does not have a lid, although *The Sensible Cook* provides several exceptions to this rule. In modern Dutch usage, the term is also used for cake.

Tansy: Tanacetum vulgare (the young, tender leaves are made into egg fritters in the spring).

Trammel: long pothook which can be adjusted up or down.

Verjuice: juice from unripe grapes.

Vla, **sometimes** *vlade,* **or** *vla(a)y:* the word has a dual meaning of custard or thin porridge; and a round flat pie.

Bibliography

Anonymous. Van Cortlandt Family Cookbook, 1865. Historic Hudson Valley, Tarrytown, N.Y.

Baart, Jan; Mario Fraenkel; Jacques Giele; Henk van Nierop; and Lucas Reijnders. *Brood, Aardappels en Patat.* Edited by Renee Kistemaker and Carry van Lakerveld. Purmerend: Amsterdams Historisch Museum MUUSSES, 1983.

Battus, Carolus. *Eenen Seer Schonen/ende Excellenten Coc-boeck.... 2d ed.* Dordrecht, 1593.

Belden, Louise Conway. *The Festive Tradition.* New York: Norton, 1983.

Braudel, Fernand. *Capitalism and Material Life 1400 – 1800.* Translated by Miriam Kochan. New York: Harper and Row, 1967.

Brown, Christopher. " ... *Niet Ledighs of Ydels.* ... " Amsterdam: J. H. de Bussy, 1984.

Buisman, G. *Practisch Handboek voor den Brood- en Banketbakker.* 3d ed. Amsterdam: N.V. Uitgevers-Maatschappij V/H Van Mantgem & De Does, 1946.

Burema, Lambertus. *De Voeding in Nederland van de Middeleeuwen tot de Twintigste Eeuw.* Assen: Van Gorcum, 1953.

Carson, Jane. *Colonial Virginia Cookery.* 2d ed. Williamsburg: The Colonial Williamsburg Foundation, 1985.

D'Allemagne, Henry Rene. *Decorative Antique Iron Work.* New York: Dover, 1968.

Davies, D. W. *A Primer of Dutch Seventeenth Century Overseas Trade.* The Hague: Martinus Nijhoff, 1961.

[De Bonnefons, Nicholas]. *Le Jardinier François.* Paris: n.p., 1692.

Deetz, James. *In Small Things Forgotten.* Garden City, N.Y.: Anchor Press, 1977.

De Kleyn, J. *Pot-sierlijk.* Arnhem: Nederlands Openluchtmuseum, 1977.

De Peyster, Anna. Handwritten cookbook. Historic Hudson Valley, Tarrytown, N.Y.

De Vries, Jan. *The Dutch Rural Economy in the Golden Age, 1500 – 1700.* New Haven: Yale Univ. Press, 1974.

Dilliard, Maud Esther. *An Album of New Netherland.* New York: Bramhall House, 1963.

Duval, Emile. *Moderne Suikerbakkerij.* Willebroek: 'Gust Convent, 1946.

Fitchen, John. *The New World Dutch Barn: A Study of Its Characteristics, Its Structural System, and Its Probable Erectional Procedures.* Syracuse: Syracuse Univ. Press, 1968.

Folkerts, Jan. "Kiliaen Van Rensselaer and the Agricultural Productivity in His Domain: A New Look at the First Patroon and Rensselaerswijck before 1664." Paper delivered at Rensselaerswyck Seminar, Albany, 1986.

Forbes, W. A. *De Oudhollandse Keuken.* Bussum: Van Dishoeck, n.d.

Funk, Elisabeth Paling. "Washington Irving and His Dutch-American Heritage as Seen in "A History of New York," "The Sketch Book," "Bracebridge Hall," and "Tales of a Traveller." Fordham Univ., 1986.

Glasse, Hannah. *The Art of Cookery Made Plain and Easy.* 1st American ed. Hamden: Archon Books, 1971.

Grant, Anne. *Memoirs of an American Lady.* 1901. Reprint. Freeport, N.Y.: Books for Libraries Press, 1972.

Grider, Rufus A. Notebook, 1888, vol. 8, Rufus A. Grider Collection. New York State Library, Albany.

Hamlin, Mrs. Charles S. "Some Remembrances," 1928 and 1929. McKinney Library, Albany Institute of History and Art, Albany.

Hess, Karen. *Martha Washington's Booke of Cookery.* New York: Columbia Univ. Press, 1981.

Irving, Washington. *A History of New York.* Edited by Edwin T. Bowden. New York: Twayne Publishers, 1964.

Irving, Washington. "The Legend of Sleepy Hollow." *The Sketch Book of Geoffrey Crayon, Gent. The Complete Works of Washington Irving.* Vol. 8. Edited by Haskell S. Springer. Boston: Twayne Publishers, 1978.

Kalm, Peter. *Travels in North America: The English Version of 1770.* Edited by Adolph B. Benson. 2 vols. New York: Dover, 1966.

Kellar, Jane Carpenter; Ellen Miller; and Paul Stambach, comp. and ed. *On the Score of Hospitality.* Rev. ed. Albany: Historic Cherry Hill, 1986.

Kennedy, William. *O Albany!* New York: Penguin, 1983.

Kenney, Alice P. *The Gansevoorts of Albany: Dutch Patricians in the Upper Hudson Valley.* Syracuse: Syracuse Univ. Press, 1969.

———. *Stubborn for Liberty: The Dutch in New York.* Syracuse: Syracuse Univ. Press, 1975.

Kistemaker, Renee; Michiel Wagenaar; and Jos van Assendelft. *Amsterdam Marktstad.* Amsterdam: Dienst van het Marktwezen, 1984.

Kouwenhoven, John A. *The Columbia Historical Portrait of New York.* Garden City, N.Y.: Doubleday, 1953.

Luiken, Jan. *Het Menselijk Bedrijf.* Translated by A. ten Cate Houwink. Haarlem: H. J. W. Becht, 1987.

Nannings, J. H. *Brood- en Gebakvormen en hunne Beteekenis in de Folklore.* Reprint. The Hague: n.p., n.d.

Nooter, Eric, and Patricia U. Bonomi, eds. *Colonial Dutch Studies.* New York: New York Univ. Press, 1988.

O'Callaghan, E. B., comp. and trans. *Laws and Ordinances of New Netherland, 1638–1674.* Albany: Weed, Parsons, 1868.

"Port Records." London: Public Record Office. Typescript. Historic Hudson Valley, Tarrytown, N.Y.

Price, J. L. *Culture and Society in the Dutch Republic During the 17th Century.* New York: Scribner, 1974.

Randolph, Mary. *The Virginia Housewife.* Edited by Karen Hess. Columbia: Univ. of South Carolina Press, 1984.

Rink, Oliver A. *Holland on the Hudson.* Ithaca: Cornell Univ. Press, 1986.

Schama, Simon. *The Embarrassment of Riches.* New York: Knopf, 1987.

Scholte-Hoek, C. H. A. *Het Gastmaal en de Tafel.* Amsterdam: Elsevier, n.d.

Schotel, G. D. J. *De Hollandsche Keuken en Kelder uit de 17e Eeuw.* Leiden: A. W. Sijthoff, n.d.

Segal, Sam. *A Prosperous Past: the Sumptuous Still Life in the Netherlands 1600–1700.* Edited by William B. Jordon. The Hague: S. D. U. Publishers, 1988.

Sels, Hilde, with Jozef Schildermans. "De Verstandige Kok," *Academie voor de Streekgebonden Gastronomie* 2 (April 1988):7–187.

Sloane, Eric. *An Age of Barns.* Edited by Alan Ternes. New York: The American Museum of Natural History, 1976.

Stam-Dresselhuys, J. P., and J. C. Wessels-Nijenhuis. *Oudnederlandse Streekrecepten.* 6th ed. Ede, The Netherlands: Zomer & Keuning, 1981.

Stevenson, Anne, and Magdalena Douw. Handwritten cookbook. Historic Hudson Valley, Tarrytown, N.Y.

Ter Molen, J. R.; A. P. E. Ruempol; and A. G. A. van Dongen, eds. *Huisraad van een Molenaarsweduwe.* Amsterdam: De Bataafse Leeuw, 1987.

Van de Graft, Catharina. *Nederlandse Volksgebruiken bij Hoogtijdagen.* Rev. ed. Edited with an Introduction by Tjaard W. R. de Haan. Utrecht: Het Spectrum, 1978.

Van der Donck, Adriaen. *A Description of the New Netherlands.* Edited with an Introduction by Thomas F. O'Donnell. Syracuse: Syracuse Univ. Press, 1968.

Van der Groen, Jan; P. Nijland; and Anonymous. *Het Vermakelijck Landtleven.* Amsterdam: Gysbert de Groot, 1683.

Vander Noot, Thomas. *Een Notable Boecxke van Cokerije. . . .* Brussels: n.p. [1510].

Van der Zee, Henri and Barbara. *A Sweet and Alien Land*. New York: Viking, 1978.

Van Deursen, A. Th. *Het Kopergeld van de Gouden Eeuw*. Vol. 1. Assen: Van Gorcum, 1981.

Van Hinte, Jacob. *Netherlanders in America*. Grand Rapids, Mich.: Baker, 1985.

Van Hoeven, Wilma. *Streekgerechten uit Nederland*. Utrecht: Spectrum, 1983.

Van Laer, A. J. F. trans. and ed. *Minutes of the Court of Fort Orange and Beverwyck*. Vol. 1. Albany: Univ. of the State of New York, 1920.

Van Lamoen, Jo. *Van Hete Bliksem en Prauwels*. Baarn, The Netherlands: In den Toren, 1987.

Van 't Veer, Annie. *Oud-Hollands Kookboek*. 2d ed. Utrecht: Spectrum, 1981.

Van Winter, Johanna Maria. *Van Soeter Cokene*. Haarlem: Fibula Van Dishoeck, 1976.

Wabeke, Bertus Harry. *Dutch Emigration to North America, 1624 – 1860*. New York: The Netherlands Information Bureau, 1944.

Wannee, C. J. *Kookboek van de Amsterdamse Huishoudschool*. Edited by R. Lotgering-Hillebrand. 17th ed. Amsterdam: Becht, n.d.

Ward, Barbara McLean, and Gerald W. R. Ward, eds. *Silver in American Life*. New York: American Federation of Arts, 1979.

Wheaton, Barbara Ketcham. *Savoring the Past*. Philadelphia: Univ. of Pennsylvania Press, 1983.

Wilcoxen, Charlotte. *Dutch Trade and Ceramics in America in the Seventeenth Century*. Albany: Albany Institute of History and Art, 1987.

———. *Seventeenth Century Albany: A Dutch Profile*. Rev. ed. Albany: Albany Institute of History and Art, 1984.

Witteveen, J. "Van Trinolet tot Ragout," *Nederlands Tijdschrift voor Dietisten* 36 (May 1981):170–75.

Reference Works

De Vries, J. *Etymologisch Woordenboek*. Rev. ed. P. L. M. Tummers. Utrecht: Het Spectrum, 1979.

Montagne, Prosper. *Larousse Gastronomique*. Edited by Charlotte Turgeon and Nina Froud. New York: Crown, 1961.

Sewel, W. *A Large Dictionary English and Dutch in Two Parts*. Amsterdam: Evert Visscher, Boekverkooper, 1727.

Skeat, Walter W. *A Concise Etymological Dictionary of the English Language*. New York: G. P. Putnam's Sons, 1980.

Van Dale Groot Woordenboek der Nederlandse Taal. 2 vols. 10th ed.

Van Dale Groot Woordenboek Engels-Nederlands. 1984 ed.

Van Dale Groot Woordenboek Nederlands-Engels. 1986 ed.

Index

(References to Recipes for Modern Kitchens are in **bold face type**.)

THE SENSIBLE COOK

was composed in 11 on 13 Sabon on a Mergenthaler Linotron 202
by Partners Composition;
printed by sheet-fed offset on 60-pound, acid-free Glatfelter Natural Hi Bulk,
Smyth-sewn and bound over binder's boards in Holliston Roxite C
by Braun-Brumfield, Inc.;
with dust jackets printed in 2 colors
by Braun-Brumfield, Inc.;
designed by Mary Peterson Moore;
and published by

SYRACUSE UNIVERSITY PRESS
SYRACUSE, NEW YORK 13244-5160